THE OLD-TIME
RIVER RATS

Tales of Bygone Days
along the Wild Mississippi

KENNY SALWEY

Voyageur Press

First published in 2009 by Voyageur Press, an imprint of MBI Publishing
Company, 400 First Avenue North, Suite 300, Minneapolis, MN 55401 USA

Voyageur Press titles are also available at discounts in bulk quantity for industrial or
sales-promotional use. For details write to Special Sales Manager at MBI Publishing
Company, 400 First Avenue North, Suite 300, Minneapolis, MN 55401 USA.

To find out more about our books, visit us online at www.voyageurpress.com.

Library of Congress Cataloging-in-Publication Data

Salwey, Kenny, 1943–
    The old-time river rats : tales of bygone days along the wild Mississippi / Kenny
Salwey.
      p. cm.
    ISBN 978-0-7603-3497-3 (plc)
    1. Mississippi River Valley—Social life and customs. 2. Mississippi River
Valley—Social conditions. 3. River life—Mississippi River Valley—History. 4.
Country life—Mississippi River Valley—History. 5. City and town life—
Mississippi River Valley—History. 6. Mississippi River—History. I. Title.
    F355.S25 2009
    977'.033092—dc22
                                    2009000594

Edited by Danielle Ibister
Designed by Barbara Drewlo
Cover designed by Elly Rochester

Printed in the United States

Cover, pages 1 and 10: Photos provided by La Crosse Magazine, *published by
Mueller Media, Inc., La Crosse, WI, Bruce Defries, Photographer*
Page 2: Courtesy of Tom Kelley, U.S. Fish and Wildlife Service
Page 8: Courtesy of Mark J. Ness, Chicago

This book is dedicated to

TERRY JUDD, *my brother-in-law and friend. Terry was a man who understood the pleasures of nature far better than most.*

DAVEY KUNDA, *my very first "kid" I took under my wing over forty years ago.*

JIM FORSTER, *a good friend and fellow believer in young folks and the need for them to experience nature.*

SMOKEY JIM STOKES *of the Dakota people, my longtime friend and mentor who married Mary Kay and me in a blanket ceremony.*

All of these folks have passed over to the other side during the last year. Each of them loved and respected the natural world. They will be sorely missed and remembered for as long as the robin sings and the green grass grows with the coming of spring, by me and all their fellow travelers in the great Circle of Life.

CONTENTS

ACKNOWLEDGMENTS

Many thanks to Orlin and Kathy Brommer and to Dick and Ginny Brommerich for their help regarding the story of Ott and Ann found in this book.

I say thank you so very much to a pair of fine friends and excellent professional photographers whose photos appear in this book: Sandra Lines, who works out of Winona, Minnesota, and Mark J. Ness, based in Chicago, Illinois.

A special thank you goes to my editor, Danielle Ibister. Danielle has the amazing talent of being able to make sense of my handwritten scribblings. She is long on patience and short on criticism. What a pleasure to work with you, Danielle!

INTRODUCTION

In the upper reaches of the Mississippi River Valley, high rugged hills stand guard like ancient watchmen on both sides of the Big River. To the west of the main river channel lies Minnesota; to the east, Wisconsin.

The hills bathe their feet in the river. Then they rise sharply to form deep ravines and steep sides studded with red, black, and white oak trees. Hickory, basswood, elm, popple, and white birch join their neighbors. Close to the ground grow many kinds of shrubs and saplings. In places, the tops of trees lie scattered about, leftovers from logging operations. Berry bushes grow thick as the hair on a dog. Prickly ash lies in wait to clutch at your clothes.

At times, the hillsides are so steep that one must hang on to the trees to keep from sliding into the deep ditches at the bottom of the ravine. It helps to follow game trails. Critters generally take the path of least resistance. However, to travel the hill country is still a far cry from a walk in the park.

In fact, there is a standing joke among hill folk. If you want to live in the hills, you need to be a "side hill gouger." A side hill gouger is a person who has one leg shorter than the other; therefore, he can walk on a side hill on a fairly level plane as long as the short leg is on the uphill side. The problem is that he can only go around the hill in one direction. There ain't no way of gettin' back again.

The crowning glory of the hilltops are huge, craggy limestone and sandstone cliffs from which a person could tumble hundreds of feet into the wooded hillside below. I have often sat on these outcroppings and pretended I was a red-tailed hawk or an eagle soaring over the great river valley. The sounds of life find my ears: A train track and a highway on each side of the river. A towboat churning its way upstream. The far-off bark of a dog. The rap of a woodpecker in the woods.

The feel of the homeless hilltop winds is soft across my cheek, and the smell of the river bottoms and the woods below is drifting upon it. Across and up and down, I can see forever until the distant landscape becomes a blur of blue-gray shadows.

This is a place where thoughts run deep and dreams drift easily to and fro. I touch the timeless stones and wonder, how long have they been here? How long will they last? Who has touched them before or will again?

The very tops of the hills are much flatter. A gentle roll envelops the land. Here the earth has been cleared of trees and is tilled for crops. Small farmsteads dot the landscape. These open agricultural hilltops are called ridges. Some are a few hundred yards wide; others are several miles across. All are named: Canada Ridge, Belvidere Ridge, Alma Ridge, Grasshopper Ridge.

Once you cross a ridge, you again find yourself in dense woodland heading downhill. You also find yourself facing the same degrees of grade as on the other side of the hill: steep, steeper, and steepest.

Now we are finally at the bottom of the hill. The land here has been cleared and is not as rolling as the ridges, so the farms are larger. These places are called valleys and each one also has a name: Eagle Valley, Yeager Valley, Waumandee Valley, Daley's Valley, Rose Valley.

In most valleys, crystal-clear spring waters bubble and gurgle out of the earth. These waters come from underground rivers and pools, and they are born to daylight at a constant temperature of around fifty degrees Fahrenheit, making them cool in the summertime and warm in the wintertime.

The spring waters make their way down through the valley, picking up depth and volume from other springs that trickle from nooks and crannies here and there. In correct English, these combined waters would now be called a "creek." However, all the hill folk and river rats I've ever known have always called it a "crick." No matter what it is called, it is a beautiful thing to behold.

Now the crick skirts the end of a cornfield. Then it flows through a sun-dappled meadow and meanders into a shady pasture. Here, I sit in the shadow of an old cottonwood, where the crick dallies awhile in an open pool. My thoughts are of the happy, sparkling waters in the crick before me. They are youthful, fresh waters, just newborn a ways up the valley. Yet, on the other hand, they are very old, as old as time itself. These waters have been here before. They have made the great circle of all the rivers of the world.

I ponder the questions: How many times have they coursed down this valley, past this tree, past me? Have I seen this water rise in a heavy mist from the Big River in autumn? Have I felt it as soothing raindrops running off my hat brim to fall into the parched mouth of the hot summer's dust? Or did it sift down through the naked treetops to cover my old wool mackinaw coat and the earth as the first winter's snow? Have I seen it with the coming of spring, rampaging down the hillside ravines as runoff, and nothing could stop it from joining the cricks again?

I think of the countless generations of trout nourished and sheltered by the cold, fast-flowing cricks. They are beautiful, wary, graceful fish that cannot live in other waters.

Slowly, my mind turns to the old-timers with whom I've shared such places. There were dogs, fish, other critters, and people. A passing parade of beings. Of memories. Like the waters of the crick, they have gone downstream. Yet they will always remain with me.

The crick continues down the valley. Like all youthful things, it is full of zest and seems impatient to get where it's going, to experience life. It dances and twists its way downstream, until it joins other cricks from a host of valleys formed by row after row of hills, which run inland twenty-five miles from the Mississippi River.

Now the cricks become small rivers, coursing down wider valleys like those of the Chippewa, Buffalo, Trempealeau, and Black rivers in Wisconsin. On the Minnesota side, the Root, Zumbro, and Minnesota rivers do likewise. All of these rivers are tributaries of the Mississippi. And all of the cricks have assumed a new identity with new characteristics. Gone are the days of youthful, happy dancing through peaceful cornfields, meadows, and pastures. Bubbling enthusiasm is a thing of the past. The pace of the waters slows considerably. There is much work to be done. Tons upon tons of silt must be moved. The silt presents an obstacle to the water's natural flow, and each tiny kernel must be pushed to the side or rolled downstream. It is a never-ending task.

There is a whole new set of critters and birds and fish and people to sustain. Instead of crick chubs, suckers, and trout, there are carp, catfish, and smallmouth bass to shelter and feed.

I use my walking stick as I move along the bank of the river. There are many beaver slides and much cutting of willows. White-tailed deer have made deeply rutted trails to the water. River otter toilets are piled a half-foot high with fish scales and bones. Raccoon tracks cover the sandbars. Trees have been torn out by their roots from windstorms or spring floods. Under the upturned roots, a mink has been hunting for frogs. A huge logjam lies in deep water on the inside of a sweeping curve. Entire trees are submerged in a watery grave. Others jut out of the water, at all angles, ten feet or more into the air. A whole lot of driftwood is tangled in the midst of the jam.

I stop to marvel at the power of the waters now that the cricks have joined forces. It is a dangerous place. The current seems angry and treacherous. One would not want to fall in here!

Across from the logjam on a sandbar, a pair of Canada geese calmly preens. High in the sky, a red-tailed hawk turns effortlessly in wide circles.

When the waters of these small rivers lived separately as cricks, their relationship with people was much different.

Once in a while, a trout angler would slip along the bank to cast his line or sit beneath a shade tree. On a hot summer's day, a couple of kids might wile away an afternoon wading barefoot in the clear, cool water. Now and then, a farmer would come down to the crick to herd his cows back to the barn for the evening milking. Limited contact, to say the least.

As a small river, however, the people traffic has been cranked up a few notches. Hunters and anglers, birders and hikers travel its banks. Canoes and kayaks and small boats powered by outboard motors go upstream and down, back and forth, to and fro.

The waters of the small rivers cannot stop to ponder their circumstances. They have a destination in mind, a commitment to fulfill. They must roll on until they emerge between the Ancient Watchmen Hills to once again change their identity. The waters have made the big time now. They have blended with the mighty Mississippi, the third-longest river in the world. It drains more than one million square miles—parts of thirty-two states and two Canadian provinces. It is a world-class resource.

The Mississippi is sometimes called Old Man River. Also the Lazy River. It is both and, as they say, much, much more. In this new partnership, the waters we have followed—youthful and impatient, busy and overworked—finally get some well-deserved rest and relaxation. Old Man River moves along at a slow, deliberate pace. He often stops to rest a bit—to catch his breath, so to speak.

During the open-water seasons of the year—spring, summer, and fall—the main channel of the Big River is a busy, hectic place. Pleasure boats of all kinds, runabouts, flatbottoms, pontoon boats, bass boats, and even small yachts and big, long houseboats tool up and down this deep-water channel. Huge diesel-powered towboats push tows made up of as many as fifteen barges that stretch hundreds of feet long. Buoys and mile markers show where the channel is located. Around the clock, the channel bears traffic.

Off to the sides, away from the main channel, is where the Lazy River dwells. Here is where the waters kick back and spread out, at times for miles, toward the Watchmen Hills lining the Big River valley. These areas are called backwaters or river bottoms. Most river folk refer to these places as the bottoms or the swamp.

Here you will find a myriad of islands, ponds, marshes, and sloughs. The islands sport trees like swamp white oak, river birch, green ash, silver maple, and cottonwood. There are quite a few small willow and red dogwood. Ground cover consists of sedge grasses, a couple of kinds of ferns, and poison ivy. Balls of fire, is there poison ivy! Small fields of it stand at the ready, waiting for the innocent and unwary. As if that isn't enough, the dreaded stuff climbs up the tree trunks as well. This is no place to saunter about wearing a short-sleeve shirt, short pants, and sandals, or you just might end up itchin' to sing a chorus of the poison ivy blues like you ain't never done before.

The islands generally run north and south or, to put it another way, upstream to downstream. They come in all manner of shapes and sizes. Some islands may be only a half acre; others could be more than forty acres. Most do not stand more than six feet above the normal water line. Other islands have almost no banks whatsoever. All are covered with water during a flood when Old Man River becomes angry.

The ponds, marshes, and sloughs are veritable water gardens. Wild rice, cattails, water lotus, pickerel weed, water lilies, bulrushes, and arrowhead flourish in the shallow waters.

This is also the home of that black, boot-suckin' Mississippi mud. Eons of decaying vegetation is what manufactures it. When you're walking through it wearing rubber knee boots, all of a sudden you get a funny feeling in one foot. You turn around and there stickin' in the mud is one of your rubber knee boots. It sucked the boot plumb off your foot.

Critters abound in the bottoms and swamps: white-tailed deer, possum, raccoon, tree squirrel , mink, beaver, and river otter, to name a few. The Mississippi flyway is one of the greatest migration routes in the world for waterfowl, shorebirds, songbirds, and hawks and eagles. Great horned and barred owls are permanent residents. And fish. Oh, are there fish! Catfish, carp, sheepshead, bullhead, small- and largemouth bass, northern pike, walleye, yellow perch, sunfish, crappie, and a great many more. There's tons of turtles, legions of frogs, and swarms of insects galore. The swamps and river bottoms are the nurseries for all the wild things that live in or along the Big River corridor.

This was the kind of country where I eked out a living as a river rat for more than three decades in a place called Whitman Swamp. There are over six thousand acres here to roam. It's home to me.

A couple of my old shacks are still down in that swamp. The Marsh Shack sets a ways out in the middle of the swamp, so I don't get there as much as I'd like anymore. However, Big Lake Shack, nestled on the Wisconsin side, makes for easier visits on my part.

Well, my friend, we've traveled together for quite a ways, haven't we now?

We've climbed the Big River side of the Watchmen Hills, where goats would find it a strain. Then we crossed the ridge and sallied forth down the backside of the hill to the valley. Here we observed the bubbling rebirth of the waters and danced and meandered with them, until they joined forces with others of their kin to form a small river.

We commiserated with the small river over its loss of innocence and youth and the heavy workload it now faced. These middle-aged waters were now compromised, less clear, and slower. They surged on, however, relentlessly pushing toward a destination that only they seemed to know. On they went, down through a wider, nonetheless beautiful, hill country valley to merge with Old Man River—and so did we.

There was so much to experience in that vast river valley. It took time and so did we.

Life along the main channel was examined. We wandered into the swamps and river bottoms among the islands and ponds and sloughs and marshes. There we rubbed elbows with the critters and the birds, the plants and the fish, the trees and the mud.

Finally we have come to my old home, Big Lake Shack in the Whitman Swamp. We pull the rusty railroad spike from between two nails and open the creaky door. Our breath catches the aroma of waste-oil-soaked boards, various herbs, a thousand wet dogs, wood smoke, and mice.

I crank up the old woodstove and set a fire-blackened pot of tea upon it to simmer.

You stand and gape at objects that make up your surroundings. Some are functional, like the kitchen utensils on the north wall and the bedrolls and clothes on the four bunks. Then there are the guns, axes, splitting mauls, walking sticks, and ice chisels standing against the wall studs. All the studs and rafters are uncovered. However, it is the ceiling hanging full of turtle shells, sweet grass, ginseng plants, a turkey beard, morel mushrooms, a two-dollar bill, and other assorted valuables that has riveted your attention.

Come on. Take a seat across from me. Move the kerosene lamp to the side and rest your elbows on the soiled oak plank table.

You see, the reason we've been traveling together is 'cause the Mississippi River Valley and the surrounding hill country is where I was born and raised and have lived for the past sixty-five years. I'd like to share some of my life with you if you're up to it. So it's good if you know the lay of the land around here.

Go ahead. Kick back. Life's too short to hurry through it. In the end, there are only memories.

We'll raise a glass to the old-timers and the places and times that were.

I'll tell you how it was.

Ann and Ottmar Probst, 1924.
Courtesy of Kathy Brommer

Part I

River Rats

The muskrat was their namesake. Like the muskrat, "people" river rats were wild critters. They were hard to domesticate and rarely seen in confined quarters. They had within them a free and independent spirit that was unflappable, and they were as stubborn as a hog on ice.

The old-timers were as tough as baling wire. Bend them one way and they'd spring back the other way. There was simply no way to keep the "bent" in any one position. Perhaps this was because their activities were always changing with the seasons of the year and the moods of the Big River.

In the spring after the ice went out, most river rats put out set lines. This required a commercial set line license, bought from the state Department of Natural Resources. Each person was allowed to set out four heavy cord lines with one hundred hooks attached to each line, baited with beef blood, clam meat, cut-up dogfish, or other assorted delicacies. The goal was to catch "rough" fish, such as bullheads, channel catfish, and mudcats (a common name for flathead catfish). The fish were sold by the pound to local fish markets. A higher price was paid for cleaned fish; a lower price was paid for uncleaned fish, or fish "in the round."

The fish market would ice down the fish and ship semi-trucks full from the backwaters of the Mississippi River to cities like Chicago and New York City. In those days, most sizeable river towns had their own fish market. Today, they have gone the way of the river rat.

Some rats engaged in gill netting and seining hauls for carp. Sheepshead and buffalo fish also were sold to the fish markets by the pound.

Here and there along the Big River, families sold fresh and smoked fish directly from their homes. Some even had regular, once-a-week routes whereby they delivered their goods to the nearby hill folk and to hill country stores and saloons in various dusty crossroad villages.

Then, too, in the summer, there was turtle trapping. Snapping turtles were caught in wire cages baited with aged fish. The turtles were sold for their meat.

At regular intervals during the spring and summer, the whole family would fish with hook and line, mostly baited with worms and minnows, in order to catch sunfish, bass, northern pike, perch, and walleye. Game fish such as these had to be released when caught on set lines, gill nets, or seine hauls. The family of river rats ate what they could catch on a fishing pole, so that they could sell the rough fish caught commercially.

With the coming of autumn, fishing ceased and hunting began, duck hunting in particular. Every rat family had some sort of water dog sleeping under a shade tree or lounging under the front porch all summer long, just hanging out until fall. The dog might be a springer spaniel, a black or yellow Labrador retriever, an Irish water spaniel, a Chesapeake Bay retriever, a combination of the above—or just a mutt off the street who happened to enjoy swimming, riding in a boat, the sound of gunshots, the smell of ducks, and the spotlight shining upon them as they brought back a duck to their friend waiting in a blind or the homemade wooden strip boat beached on a backwater island. Ducks were roasted, fried, made into stews and soups, and smoked with hickory wood, plus put up in glass jars.

Winter brought trapping time. Muskrats were the bread and butter of the trap line. They were fairly easy to catch and not too difficult to skin, flesh, and stretch. They usually commanded an acceptable price per fur.

Beaver, mink, and raccoon were also caught and sold. Come spring, the average river rat family was none too happy because their larder was empty and their pocketbook was as flat as a pancake layin' on a busy highway. The whole cycle began again, and everything depended on the weather.

River rats had a certain look about them. Most dressed in "everyday clothes" every day of the week—including Sunday. They sported a permanent tan, summer and winter. Time spent outdoors in all seasons will do that, you know. Their hands were as calloused and rough as sandpaper. At times, when I shook hands with a river rat, I winced. They were unaware of their own strength. Most were shy and polite in public, especially around girls and women, even though women were as much a part of river rat life as men. River rats had scars—scars everywhere from using knives and axes and ice chisels and traps in their daily work.

At times, a river rat was forced to defend his territory against invaders in an out-and-out, knockdown, drag-out fistfight. This usually occurred in a saloon or dance hall after the combatants had tasted a little fermented fruit of the vine. However, some of these confrontations took place right where the infringement occurred: on a windswept icepack, a remote backwater, or a steep wooded hillside. There were those rats who were known for their quick fists, hard chins, and hot tempers. Isn't that the way of all wild things? They all compete for territory. It is nature's way.

The old-timers, hill folk, and river rats alike ate the kind of things that would give today's dieticians and medical doctors recurring nightmares. Diets, calories, saturated fats, and cholesterol meant absolutely nothing to them.

Today, the true old-time river rat lifestyle has pretty much disappeared. Oh, yes, one can still find a few rats scattered along the upper Mississippi. However, they are all fifty years of age on up. Young ones won't generally be found. The river rat lifestyle is just too unpredictable, is too much hard work, and cannot generate enough income to support a modern-day family's expectations. Some youngsters dabble a bit in the old ways for extra money. However, the true dyed-in-the-wool, completely-dependent-upon-the-river-and-hills rat is gone.

I believe it is of paramount importance to record the life and times of these extraordinary people. I was a young, budding river rat when the old-timers were still around. I had the distinct honor and privilege of living and working among them. As you read these stories, please try to remember that their wit and intelligence were second to none. Their colloquial talk—and mine—simply reflects the genuine fact that the edges of our vocabulary had never been smoothly shaped by the grinding wheel of higher education.

So, my friends, I share these river rat stories with you in the only way I know how: from up close and personal experience.

1. Ott and Ann

My hand felt like it was clamped into a supersized bench vise. "How ya doin', old timer?" I asked through clenched teeth.

"Oh, not too bad for the shape I'm in," replied the white-haired old man. He pumped my arm up and down before releasing his viselike grip.

I let my hand hang loose against my side and worked it around some to get feeling back, while the old man and I exchanged complaints about how hot it was. He suggested we should find us a shade tree in the backwaters and do some fishin' under it. I agreed and followed him from the yard in front of his small riverside house, across the road, and down a set of rickety wooden steps.

He had a most peculiar habit when walking. About every six or eight steps, without interrupting his stride, he would briefly rub the face of one shoe across the back of the opposite pant leg. He always claimed that was his method of shining his shoes.

I was walking in the shadow of a living river rat legend.

The name Ottmar Probst was known for many miles up and down the Big River and far into the surrounding hills as well. I called him Ott, to which he sometimes objected, saying, "It sounds too much like 'odd' to suit me, although I reckon that ain't so awful far from the truth!"

He was a big man, rawboned and square-shouldered with not an ounce of fat on him. Early photos of Ott liken him to the movie star George Clooney. However, if Ott were living today, he would insist it was the other way around.

Ott's voice was deep and resonant, like a bullfrog. His eyes twinkled and sparkled. Always a hearty laugh was waiting to crease the lines in his face. In keeping with those who have a kind sense of humor, Ott laughed longest and hardest at his own misadventures—which were many, to say the least! It was, however, his hands that caught one's instant attention. His palms were wider than the average china saucer. His gnarled, scarred fingers called to mind Polish sausages left on the table overnight. Even in his older years, Ott possessed bone-crunching power in his hands, arms, and shoulders.

Most times when meeting folks, Ott presented a gruff and growly, rough-and-ready exterior. Some he intrigued; others he scared. However, if a person was fortunate enough to spend a fair amount of time with him and coupled that with a little patience, his underlying character of kindness, decency, and peacefulness became transparent.

He was difficult to understand at times, for a couple of reasons. The first of which was the way he pronounced the letters "g" and "j." Both sounded like "ch" as in "children." In his own words, he explained it best: "I'm only the second cheneration of Chermans in this country." Or: "Chesus, but it's cold outside today." Then there was Ott's daughter-in-law, Ginny. Ott would often say, "Ya know somethin', Kenny, that Chinny is a pretty darn good woman."

The second reason was Ott's self-described "lack of school-housing." He told me, "Now and then I went to the little brick schoolhouse that used to set up on the bank alongside of Lizzy

Paul's Pond till I got big enough to help Pa on our little ole sand burr farm up the river here a piece."

Ott would look at me to see if he had my attention. He needn't have worried. I was all ears, for I fully understood that this old river rat had already forgotten more about the Big River than I would ever know.

He continued, "See, I was born in 1901, and there weren't much for doctors 'round here them days. Was one in Alma. By the time Pa rowed his homemade wooden boat the eight or ten miles upriver to Alma, rounded up ole doc, and brung 'im on back home, there was trouble here. My head'd been hanging out for quite a spell. Ma was havin' trouble birthin' me. Weren't her only trouble, though. Poor woman had to pass water, couldn't hold it no more, so she did. Some of it must'a run up my nose. Ma always claimed I must'a got water on my brain from it, 'cause of some of the strange ways I had from then on."

Ott stopped to see if my attention span had been stretched too far. I closed my eyes, shook my head, and mused, "So that's what caused you to be the way you are, old-timer. I always wondered how a man could get like you. Now I know. Wouldn't wanna look straight up for too long in a cloudburst either, I s'pose!"

My little dig seemed to spur him on to new heights. Ott went on, "'Nother thing about my birthin' day, young fella. It happened on the last day of October, and ya know what? To this very day and prob'ly long after I'm gone, folks dress up special and wear masks on their face and celebrate and have dancin' balls and give kids candy and all sorts of goin's on. Just on account of my birthin' day. Makes me feel real proud!

What do ya think of that, young fella? Never gonna happen to you, I'll bet my last nickel on that much!"

I knew that Ott liked a little backtalk. I quipped, "It sure won't happen to me, 'cause we weren't born on the same day, you old goat. Second thing is if bull feces was worth money, you'd be a millionaire!"

A rumble began deep in his barrel chest. It rose up and exploded in a long, hearty laugh that turned his face red and brought tears to the corners of his eyes. "Let's go up to the house and see if we kin snitch a cup of coffee off the old girl."

The "old girl" Ott referred to was his wife, Ann. At that time, they had been married for more than fifty years. Ann was a small woman with a kindly way about her that quickly put you at ease. Her crowning glory was her thick beautiful hair, white as the freshest of snowfalls. Her skin had a light olive tone. True to the fashion of those days, she most often wore a dress. Quiet and shy as she was, Ann had an inner streak of toughness. At times, Ann would rise up to make her voice heard loud and clear. She had to. After all, she had spent the better part of her life living with a snuff-chewin', hardworkin', whiskey-drinkin', rough-as-sandpaper legend of a man. A steady domestic hand was needed now and then to smooth the rough-and-tumble adventuresome waves created by her river rat husband.

As far as snitchin' coffee was concerned, not to worry! When we entered the kitchen I could smell it brewing. Ann generally had two questions to ask me: "How's everything going, Kenny?" and "Would you like a cup of coffee?"

Ott would retire to his corner kitchen table chair. Nobody else ever sat in that chair. It was Ott's, and that was that!

A small homemade cabinet hung in that corner. Inside was Ott's stash of "brandy," which was actually his home-cooked moonshine whiskey. A swig of that stuff would set your throat on fire. When it reached your belly, it seemed to explode, causing gases and fumes to rise up to your brain. This in turn created wooziness, dizziness, and loss of memory. Ott's ungodly concoction was disguised in a factory-made brandy bottle filled with his White Lightning and a few chunks of white oak charcoal to give it color.

Ott was frugal, and cooking his own whiskey was just another way of gettin' by. He took pleasure in serving an unsuspecting guest his hootch. My initial introduction to the whole process took place on a bitter cold January day. Ott and I had been out in the river bottoms checking beaver traps. By the time we returned, the trapping sled and everything in it was coated with ice. We were in the same shape. Ott asked, "Wanna come in and warm up for a minute?"

He didn't have to ask me twice. I practically pushed him through the kitchen door! We peeled off our frozen caps and coats and boots. The whole mess of beaver pelts was spread out around their woodstove to dry.

"Ah yeah, my boy," said Ott as he groaned his way into his corner chair by the kitchen table. He looked at his brandy cabinet and then looked at me. "I got a little somethin' up here what just might take the chill outta our bones. What ya think?"

I nodded. Ott reached up and opened the little cabinet door. It responded with a long, high-pitched squeak. He brought down a brandy bottle and two oversized shot glasses made of thick, heavy glass. These he carefully filled to the brim. So much so that I had to raise the glass slowly to avoid spillage.

Ott offered a toast: "Through the lips and over the gums, look out stomach, here she comes." He emptied his glass.

I followed suit, after a fashion. My first attempt resulted in me consuming a little over half of the amber liquid. By then, however, a searing fire had shut down all the working mechanisms of my throat. Breathing was next to impossible, which resulted in much coughing and gasping. Swallowing seemed beyond reach. However, a fair amount of Ott's hootch must have found its way to my stomach, for I then experienced the aforementioned eruption that quickly traveled to my brain and beyond.

I couldn't help it. Words escaped my lips, over which I had no control. "Whoa ah whee, big batches of bouncin' bunnies! What in the name of Bob did I just drink!" It wasn't a question. It was more of a statement or I s'pose English majors would say an exclamation. As I was trying to catch my breath, I glanced across the table at Ott, who sat there perfectly calm as if he'd just gulped clear water. However, I did detect, through my bleary eyes, a smirk on his face.

By then, alerted by my outburst, Ann had arrived in the kitchen. Ott turned to her and asked, as if she was some sort of journal keeper, "'Member when our preacher came here and I served him a little of my hootch?"

She nodded, and he continued: "Wall, he spat and sputtered and said some words a preacher man should never say, you know. But Kenny here hollered out some stuff I never in my life heard before, 'bout bouncin' bunnies and such. Why, he acted as if he'd done drank a gallon of kerosene or somethin'. Bet if I ran my finger behind his ears, I'd find a little water there." Ott chuckled.

I managed a lopsided grin as I shoved my less-than-half-full glass toward him. "Finish it if you want," I gasped. "It took the chill outta my bones all right. Feels like they're meltin' down right now!"

Ott promptly emptied my glass without batting an eye and sat there slowly shaking his head.

Ott and Ann's kitchen acted as the hub of all activity in the Probst household. All who came to visit ended up in the kitchen. Here, talk was exchanged about happenings along the Big River. About the wear and tear going on in the outside world. It was, however, the talk of days gone by that interested me most. Stories were told and retold. Ann and Ott were both master storytellers in their own right. All it took was a slight nudge to jar their memory and a tale would be forthcoming.

Take the time I brought a few plump, late-season mallards over to Ott and Ann's place. The November wind howled along the riverbank. Sleet spit forth from a steel-gray sky. Ott and I hunkered down, pluckin' the ducks behind one of his sheds. Ann watched us from the house.

As soon as we were through singeing the down off the ducks with a small torch, Ann stuck her head out the back door and hollered to bring the ducks into the kitchen. We'd draw 'em and wash 'em up in there. Let me tell you, it didn't take long for Ott and me to put them ducks into a five-gallon pail and make our way to the warm kitchen!

Ann had a couple of dishpans full of hot water ready. There by the woodstove, the three of us worked on the rest of the butchering job. I could see that something, however, was working on Ott's mind.

He piped up: "Know somethin', Kenny? These ducks here remind me of how I come to get the old girl."

Without looking up from the duck she was working on, Ann murmured, "Oh, so I'm gonna have to listen to that story again."

Ott winked at me. "Wall, Ann honey, I just thought it'd be nice if Kenny learned how some of us river folks got together years back when we was young, that's all."

He drew a deep breath. "See, Ann and I grew up pretty close together 'long the river here, and I always did think she was a pretty little thing. As we got growed up, we'd sometimes meet under a old weepin' willow tree next to the water. She'd make big eyes at me and toss her hair back in the breeze while the frogs was talkin' at night. I got to puttin' my arm around her and even took to kissin' her some." Ott looked at me.

I raised my eyebrows and shrugged my shoulders.

He didn't wait for me to answer. "Wall, it got to where I felt like a big ole bear sittin' by a bee tree a smackin' his lips. Had a taste of that honey and wanted more! Them days there was a spring duck season. On a day just after the ice went out, I shot ten of the nicest, fattest greenhead mallards you ever wanna see. Just like the ones we're workin' on right now, only prettier 'cause they had their spring breeding colors. I got to thinkin' to myself, Ott, you know Ann's pa, old man Hammer'd rather eat good roast duck than the finest cut of beef ever come off a cow. An idea came to me. I took up all the courage I could muster, grabbed them ducks—five in each hand—and headed for Ann's place. When I got there, I held the ducks behind me when I went into the house. There sat old man Hammer by the kitchen table."

Now Ott stopped, fished a box of Copenhagen snuff from his shirt pocket, and took a three-fingered chew. He worked the snuff carefully with his tongue, then continued: "'Pa Hammer,' I says, 'I come here today to see what you'd think about me askin' your daughter Ann to marry me.'

"It was as if I'd hit him over the knuckles with a piss elm club! He lurched back from the table and looked at me like a bulldog ready to tackle a badger. Fear struck me hard in the heart. I whipped them ten ducks out from behind me and held 'em up for the old man to see. I says, 'Pa Hammer, I brung these here ducks along for you just in case you'd say it was okay. I'd be sure to clean 'em up good and proper for the roaster 'fore I leave, too, sir.'

"Never called a whole lotta folks 'sir' but old man Hammer was one of them. His face sorta melted. Damnest thing I ever seen. Next thing I knew, I was lookin' at a big toothy smile and the old man says, 'Ann's in the other room. If it's okay with her, it's sure as Sam Hill okay with me, you young pup of a Probst!'"

Again Ott worked his snuff around some and closed his eyes as if to savor the memory of that long-ago day. "Wall, I took them ducks out on the front porch and piled 'em up nice and neat. Then I went and found Ann in the house and asked her what she thought of my plans. She didn't hesitate a minute. She says, 'I guess so.' I took that to mean yes. Musta been back in about '24, wasn't it, Ann?"

Ann said nothing. Ott continued, "Anyhow, Kenny, that's how I got the best woman in the whole wide world. Alwus was thankful to ducks for that. Still like to see 'em out in the river bottoms, remind me of that day. Grateful to 'em, a man might say."

By now, our duck-cleaning venture was finished. I could already envision the most delicious meal of wild duck ever served. Ann was the finest of cooks, and her wild duck was, as today's saying goes, to die for. Golden brown, yet tender and moist, stuffed with bread dressing, onions, celery, and sliced apples, served along with the smoothest, richest dark brown gravy you ever put a ladle into. Mashed taters and baked squash rounded out the feast. It was the kind of meal one could founder oneself at.

I carried a dishpan full of dressed ducks into the cellar to cool. Then the three of us gathered at the kitchen table for a cup of Ann's ever-present coffee.

Now Ann took up the torch. "Ott's right. It was in 1924 when we got married. Had the wedding party upriver a mile or so, where that point of land sticks out into the water. Place called Indian Point. Nowadays ain't nothin' but a bunch a cottages and fancy houses along there. Back in '24, a lot of Indian folk came up and down the river, and they'd stop along that point a ground to camp awhile. Nice folks they were. All us river rats who lived halfway close to the point knew them families that camped there. We'd trade stuff and visit back and forth together." Ann looked over the top of her glasses at Ott.

Ott offered an explanation. "See how she's lookin' at me, Kenny? Couldn't help myself at the time. Got to know the prettiest Indian girl I ever did see. Oh my, did I take a shine to her! She didn't exactly shine towards me, I guess. Was one of Frank Thunder's daughters, weren't it, Ann?"

Ann nodded and went on with her story. "Anyhow, all us neighbors, Indians, river rats, farmers, and even town folk, had us a party at Indian Point to celebrate me and Ott's gettin' married. We was neighbors all right, each and every one of us was. Everybody brought somethin' to eat and drink. And in the night I 'member under a full moon how a little band got themselves together, mostly our Indian friends, and used old fiddles, guitars, squeezeboxes, and drums and rattles to make the most beautiful music. We all danced and visited and laughed and ate and drank. I can't tell you how pretty it was. Everybody happy, together, and the moonbeams shinin' off the river, glowin' sorta golden color. Ain't seen nothin' like it since, have you, Ott?"

Ott shook his head. I detected a tear in the corner of his weathered eye. "Yup," he said, "seems like just the other day when our weddin' was." He gazed out the window at his beloved river, then mused mostly to himself, "Yah, that old man river sure does keep a movin' along."

Then the old man turned and said, "Long as you're at it, Ann, might as well tell 'im about that pretty little honeymoon cottage I had waitin' for you, don't you think?"

My attention focused on Ann. She wiped her hands on her apron and refilled our coffee cups before once again sitting down at the table. Now a sense of peace and loving remembrance settled over her.

She began: "Some honeymoon cottage that was! Kenny, I ask you, would you call a tent a honeymoon cottage? Well, Ottmar did! See, all his life, Ott picked up whatever work he could in the summertime. Carpentry, mason, workin' on farms, and such. That way he could still run set lines for catfish and trap turtles. The summer we was married, Ott had a job workin' on road construction south of here in Chicken Valley. Mostly horses was used to move the ground to make the road up through the hills. That and dynamite. And Ott knew somethin' 'bout both. So we go downriver to Chicken Valley, and there stands this wall-type tent, and Ott says, 'Honey, here's where we're gonna live for the summer!'"

She paused to look at me in order to catch my reaction. I rolled my eyes and raised my eyebrows. She did the same.

"Anyhow," she continued, "the tent was about as long as a good-sized rowboat and maybe about half that wide. Had a little woodstove in there for cookin' and for takin' the chill out of the nights. Had our clothes and dishes and such in old wooden trunks. Was a small bed that the two of us just barely fit into. Course we was young and just married, so the little bed wasn't all bad, I guess."

Ann glanced at Ott. He winked at her and grinned.

She went on. "Got our water from a spring next to the crick. Never thoughta germs and such bein' in the water, like they carry on about nowadays. Couldn't of been much to it back then, 'cause we're still here to tell about it, ain't we now?

"At first it took a little gettin' used to. After a while, the tent livin' seemed good. By the time fall come and we had to pack up and head back upriver for home, I felt bad about takin' the tent down and leavin'. I'll never forget them summer nights when the rain pitter-pattered off that tent. The frogs and crickets was talkin' and the owls was a hootin' in the woods. In the mornin' when the sun shone on the canvas, it gave off a certain smell."

Ann's eyes sparkled behind a white lock of hair hanging low across her forehead. Her lips wore a gentle smile.

Ott piped up. "Yup, I kin still feel it, too. Was one of the best summers of my life. Wish we could do the whole thing over again."

I added my two cents' worth. "Why, I guess you folks kin, alls you gotta do is keep rememberin'."

They both laughed.

In the coming years, I spent countless hours on the Big River with Ott. Wherever we went by boat, Ott insisted on doing the rowing. Oh Martha, could that man row a boat! His oars seemed to be a part of his body. Smooth, effortless strokes were repeated hour after hour, mile after mile. Upstream or down, it didn't matter, the pace was the same.

In the backwaters, where quarters were at times close, Ott could turn the boat on a dime. He'd nudge it gently against a snag to fish for sunfish or back up against the current without so much as a ripple. When handling a rowboat, Ott had the endurance of a mule, coupled with the style and grace of a gazelle.

Every now and then, however, he would bump a log or nudge a rock on a wing dam or bang against the side of his dock. At such times, he would mutter to himself and shake his head in disgust. He got down on himself for making the tiniest of errors.

Ott was truly a child of the river. He knew every deep hole, sandbar, wing dam, and submerged log for miles in every direction. He could read the water's surface like an academic would a book. Small, choppy waves meant a wing dam. Rippling lengths of water meant a sandbar. Surging, undulating currents suggested underwater logs. Whirlpools and back eddies were signs of deep, running undertows and shiftless currents. Ott reckoned with all signs in an easy, effortless manner.

The boat seemed as if it were a leaf floating upon the Big River, and Ott simply guided it along the path of least resistance. He always took the time to mention points of interest. A blue heron would evoke, "That there's the best fisher in the whole world. Got to be. Don't get nothin', their kids and them'll starve to death. Ain't like us folks goin' fishin', is it now, you young pup?"

Near dusk, a white-tailed doe followed by two fawns came to a quiet slough to quench her thirst. The doe looked up and down the slough long and hard before dimpling the water with her muzzle. Her fawns did the same. The old man whispered, "If people kids followed their ma's suit like that, there'd be a whole lot less trouble, don't ya think, Kenny?"

When passing through the autumn marshes, Ott would predict the coming winter. "Muskrats are buildin' their huts early and high in the air. Gonna be a long cold winter, you just watch and see. All critters has got a feelin' for that. We don't."

I once asked Ott how he learned to row a boat so well. He replied, "Wall, I'll tell you when I got my trainin'." He looked out across the river as if that's where the past could be found. "See, my pa, Ed Probst, had took the job of tendin' the lighthouse markers along the river channel from Buffalo City to Alma long time 'fore I was born in '01. Every one of them marker lights hada be filled up with kerosene and lit on fire 'bout dusk, so's the steamboats could tell where they was a going at night, else they'd a run aground. And they'd a been mighty displeased 'bout somethin' like that! So Pa's job was important.

"Pa made his own boats outta white oak trees. Called 'em strip boats. All narrow strips of white oak pieced together tight as he could get 'em. In the spring, he'd sink his boat all the way under the water for a week or so to swell the wood tight. When he brought 'er up, she wouldn't be so likely to leak. Made his own oars, too.

"Anyhow, Pa's job a lightin' markers made it necessary for him to do an awful lot of boat rowin'. Late afternoon, he'd load his kerosene pail and a drinkin' water jug aboard his boat and start rowin' upriver from one lighthouse to another, fillin' and lightin' the torches, as he called 'em."

Ott quit talking in order to take a dip of snuff. Then he studied his hands for a moment. "Pa started takin' me along on his nightly lightin' rounds when I was about six, maybe seven years old. Let me get a feel for the oars. Couldn't handle the boat long at first. Time I was ten or so, I was rowin' over halfway 'round our trip, mostly downstream. Pa'd always say, 'Lend your back to the oars, boy. But when you take 'em out and put 'em in, do it easy, else it's just a waste of energy. When the oars are in the water is the only time you got any power.'"

I assured Ott that his Pa had taught him well and that I'd never seen anyone row better than he did and, in all probability, never would.

Ott brought up a deep chuckle from his chest. Then he lamented, "Outboard motors has spoiled most folks when it comes to rowin' a boat. Nowadays, either they ain't never learned it proper or them that has ain't rowed in so long they's done forgot how. Boat motors cost big money to buy. Cost money to run. Somethin' busts, it costs to fix it. They're noisy, smelly things. Won't see many wild critters when you're drivin' one of them. And you talk 'bout drivin'! Wowee, Walter, do they drive them boats! Why, you'd swear they was being chased by a school of savage sharks or somethin'. On a Sunday out on the main channel, them bevies of boats are a chargin' back and forth and up and down like a herd of wild bulls. The water out there is churned to a froth. Poor river. Don't know how much more of that it kin stand."

My conversations with Ott often took place on his boat dock, which floated, after a fashion, on the quiet waters of a backwater slough. I say "after a fashion" because Ott's dock was the sort of gismo that, by all engineering standards, should not have been above the surface of the water! One could hardly believe such a structure could possibly float under any circumstances.

Now Ott was the kind of man, as were all old-time river rats, who used his native wit, intelligence, and experience to create something good and useful from what was directly at hand. Very few store-bought goods were ever used by Ott or his peers. There was a certain amount of pride involved here. "Getting by" was a large part of the lifestyle.

When it came to his dock, Ott carried this principle to the extreme. Where his dock was concerned, he was the undisputed, absolute, unequalled king of the cobblers in the river rat world. There were those who simply dropped by, especially during a springtime flood, to marvel at the fact that Ott's dock was still afloat.

You see, his dock project had begun sometime in the early to mid-1930s, shortly after he laid claim to a stretch of backwater riverbank, where he eventually built a small house. It was maybe five hundred yards from the main channel. In Ott's words, "Weren't nothin' there at all 'cept willows along the water and sand burrs up higher. So I took to cleanin' up the whole mess. Wanted to make a home place for Ann and me. First thing I done was brush out some along the water. See, every spring when the river went high, there'd be all kinds a stuff floatin' around. I went out in my boat and drug back whatever I thought could be of some kinda use. Stuff come from all over upriver. Metal barrels, old boats, and home-sawed lumber galore. Everthin' from soup to nuts jest a comin' to me everday. Got so much stuff drug in, didn't know what to do with it all. Piled it up on the riverbank. Water went down, I sorted through the pile. End of the second year, I had 'nough barrels and lumber to build me a right nice boat dock. And I did. Pretty lookin' thing it was, too."

Ott became quiet now. We were seated side by side on his dock in a pair of cast-off lawn chairs he had dredged out of the river during some long-ago flood. He was not, however, looking far off across the river toward the distant past. Rather, he was staring down at the dock under his chair. He rose, walked a few steps, bent over, and with a slight grunt picked up a peeled, weathered pole about six feet in length. This he carried to the outside edge of his dock and began to poke and fish around at various angles in the water, as if to test the depth, then bring the pole up to find the bottom of the dock.

The old man repeated this maneuver several times, then, satisfied, he turned to me with a perplexed grin. "Jest tryin' to figure out where that pretty little dock went to over the last forty years or so. It's under here someplace. I kin bet you my right butt cheek on that, Sonny!" Ott roared with laughter.

I never could quite understand whether he found such uproarious humor in the thought of his pretty little hard-earned boat dock being buried under tons of Big River flotsam or if it was the genuine fact that he would bet his right butt cheek on it. Nevertheless, Ott thoroughly vented his feelings by laughing long, hard, and hearty.

When he had gained control of himself, I queried, "Think maybe your dock is so thick 'cause you old fart couldn't stand to watch a piece of lumber float by without dragging it up on here and nailin' it down?"

Ott cleared his throat. "Now, boy, first thing is you better be careful 'bout who you're callin' an old fart, or he just might send you a rollin' off the end of this here dock and plumb into the river!" There was a twinkle in his eyes.

I nodded in agreement. We chuckled, and he continued, "Wall, I was brought up never to waste anythin', so you was right 'bout how my dock got so thick. Couldn't help myself. Hada pick up what come downriver and make some use of it. Didn't all go on the dock, though. Went and built a few sheds and lean-tos up on the high bank where the house stands now. Made mighty good use of 'em over the years. Some might call the whole thing foolish. Tell you one thing, you young pup. Never had much of a lumberyard bill to pay for. All jest kinda come to me. Other folks' loss was my gain. Still operate the same way now. Why change things when they's workin'?"

That afternoon, I helped Ott take inventory of the incredible amount of river rat tools strewn about his ever-growing dock. We sorted and piled under the soft, dense shade of a giant weeping willow. The activity gave me insight into the world of the old-time river rat, which was already then slipping quietly into the past. Everything on that dock had been gathered or foraged or somehow fashioned by Ott.

There were a half-dozen turtle hooks. These consisted of a length of iron rod, from one to three feet long, that had been heated over a forge and bent into a hook on one end. The other end was fastened to a wooden handle handcrafted from a hickory sapling. Heavy-gauge copper wire secured the rod. Turtle hooks were primarily used to find and pull turtles from their hibernaculums beneath the winter's ice pack.

Hooking turtles was, however, only one of a multitude of turtle hook uses. The hooks were also used to raise heavy, multiple-hook commercial lines set out for catfish. Turtle hooks were also used to check traps set for muskrat, mink, and beaver. In this work, the hook was pushed down along the trap stake, which was a peeled sapling that stood above the surface of the water and indicated the location of the trap. The hook caught the trap chain, and the trap and critter were brought to the surface. Of course, the retrieval of duck decoys was another practical use of turtle hooks. The hook caught the decoy's anchor cord and pulled it boatside, where the hunter could then bring the decoy aboard without dipping his hands into the ice-cold water.

Then there was the matter of hook-and-line fishing with artificial lures. Old-time river rats rarely used what they called false bait, for two reasons. First, false bait cost money they didn't have. Second, if they did have the money, they thought long and hard about spending it on something that only imitated what they already had—namely, minnows and worms. If a river rat did, however, use false baits, a turtle hook was sure to be near at hand. False baits generally sported treble hooks and were notorious for catching on submerged logs or rocks. When that happened, a few deft swipes of the turtle hook would free up the false bait, thereby saving the river rat a couple of hard-earned dollars. Some old-timers took this technique a step further by hanging around popular fishing holes. After the weekend anglers left, the river rat would carefully probe familiar underwater nooks and crannies with his trusty turtle hook to bring up false baits of every size, color, and price under the sun. The river rat would then sort through his bounty and decide which baits he would keep for himself. The rest were traded or sold to locals or, in some cases, tourists. I wonder if anyone ever recognized the fact that they were buying their own fishing lure back at a "reduced" price.

Then, too, the river rat was most times working upon the waters of the Big River. This presented a unique problem. Let's say a carpenter drops his hammer. No big deal. He picks it up off the ground and he's back in business. Not so with a river rat. He drops a hammer, an axe, a trap, a set line box, his cap, a fish box, his eyeglasses, or, God forbid, his wallet and it's goodbye, Charlie. Ain't no pickin' it up off the ground. No siree, Dudley. We got water to deal with now! What does he do? Why, as sure as the Queen of England is proper, the river rat's hand turns to the ever-present turtle hook. While never 100 percent successful, it did, however, return many a water-soaked item to an experienced "hooker" of the river rat kind!

Most times, Ott's dock was also strewn with at least three or four hatchets and axes. The handles were hand-hewn from shagbark hickory by Ott using a drawknife, plenty of time, and a whole lot of expertise and patience. He crafted as fine a homemade handle as anyone ever did anytime, anywhere. They were smooth, straight as an arrow, no gouge marks, comfortable to the hand, and in balance with the tool they were attached to, which included axes, hatchets, cant hooks, turtle hooks, cleavers, and knives. Ott's handmade handles were sought after by folks near and far.

Peeled and aged willow trap stakes lay on the monstrous dock by the hundreds in loosely tied bundles. They rested there quietly, waiting for the coming of late autumn, when they would be once again pressed into service on Ott's trap line. Their rusted and worn counterparts, the traps, were clumped in small groups held together with short pieces of wire wrapped about their chains. The traps also waited patiently to be taken to the back room of Ott's garage, where his old-time blacksmith forge was located. Here he would make each fit its intended use.

Prime furs brought another measure of self-sufficiency to Ott and Ann's life. As Ott often said, "One thing gets life from another. In a way, it's kinda a damn shame but that's the way it's always been and I reckon always will be. Ain't no way 'round the whole thing, I guess. Even when we grow a garden, it's that way. Don't matter much. It's life's way of livin'. Ya darn well katootin' it is, Sonny!"

Cages of all sizes and descriptions called Ott's dock home. Turtle traps made of two-inch-square wire mesh rested on top of one another. These would later be placed in shallow backwater ponds and lakes. Each trap had a "throat," which meant it was wide at the opening and then gradually narrower. Snapping turtles could squeeze into the interior of the cage to eat fish bait; however, they were unable to leave.

Live cages were also stacked on the dock. When Ott made a small catch of fish, whether commercially or by hook-and-line pole fishing, they were put into a live cage in the dockside waters. The live cage was fastened to the dock by way of a heavy wire or lightweight chain. When the cages held enough fish to warrant an afternoon's worth of cleaning, they were pulled up on the dock, and the fish were dressed out either for sale or for personal eating.

A myriad of miscellaneous mystery items could be found on Ott's dock as well. Only a thorough, piece-by-piece explanation by Ott himself could reveal the value of said artifacts.

Over the years, I traveled the Big River from Trempealeau, Wisconsin, all the way north to Wabasha, Minnesota, and stood alongside many an old-time river rat on his dock. But I never saw anything close to approaching Ott's dock. Yes, there were similarities; the tools of the trade were there for sure. However, the sheer multitude and magnitude of Ott's creative monstrosity were beyond comparison.

From the late 1930s to the mid-1940s, Ott tore apart an old wooden dredge and barge, both of which had been run aground and abandoned in the Big River backwaters.

Ott recalled, "Sure was an awful lotta hard work tearin' that stuff apart with sledgehammers, mauls, hand hammers, and crowbars out there in the summertime. Skeeters an' deer flies takin' their share of blood outta you. Sometime workin' in water an' mud up to the waist. Put all that there lumber—and good stuff it was too, home-sawed pine, no knots in it from the log rafts come downriver years before—into my boat. Rowed it to shore and drug it up the bank. Took all the nails out, saved 'em, and made 'em as straight as I could again. Measured things up. Sawed everthin' by hand and started buildin' a house for Ann and me. Took quite a piece of time but, by Gar, finally got 'er done. Weren't nothin' 'cept sand burrs all around it, so I started diggin' out trees from the river bottoms. Kept all the roots I could and redug 'em in 'round our house. Took a lotta pails of hand-pumped water to get 'em growin', but most of 'em did." He swept his huge hand in a broad arc across the yard.

"Ain't everbody kin say their house and everthin' round it come from there." The old-timer turned to point a Polish-sausage-sized finger at the wide, yawning expanse of islands and water lying a strong-armed stone's-throw away. The setting sun revealed satisfaction upon his weathered face.

One evening while I was sitting across from Ott at the kitchen table, he looked directly at me to gain my attention. He then turned to the small corner cabinet, winked, and slowly opened the door. A long, slow, high-pitched squeak followed the path of the door.

Before Ott could wrap his hand around his "brandy" bottle, Ann's voice was heard from a couple of rooms away: "At it again, ain't you now." It was more of a statement than a question.

Ott shook his head, took a nip from the bottle, put it back on the shelf, and closed the door.

I whispered, "Why in Sam Hill don't you oil the hinge?"

His grin was wide as he explained, "Hinge been squeakin' since I built this place. Spoil all the fun if I oiled it, don't you think, you young pup?"

I shook my head in disbelief.

"Know what, Kenny? Been drinkin' whiskey many a year now. Ain't killed me yet. Will sometime, I s'pose. Course, somethin's got to use you up. Could just as well be that, I guess."

I nodded, and Ott went on: "I was born in '01, so near as I can tell, in about '07 or so, my pa, Ed Probst, took me along into Kackering's Saloon. The place stood right where the Mississippian restaurant is now on the riverbank, 'bout halfway through Buffalo City. Them old-time saloons had a brass rail to put your feet on below the bar. There was brass spittoons along the rail every so often. Most men chewed tobacco them days and needed to spit now and then.

"Anyhow, I got in there and climbed up onto the brass rail and clenched onto the bar so's I could see over the top. The bartender had him a big, curly handlebar mustache and fancy bands round his upper arms to keep his shirt sleeves up outta his way. I 'member sayin' somethin' to 'im. He hollers down the bar to my pa, 'Hey, Ed, your kid here just ordered a shot a whiskey.' Pa never thought it over for a second. He hollers back, 'Well then give him one.' Next thing I knew, I had a shot a whiskey settin' ahead of me. Drunk it down. Been doin' so ever since.

"When I got growed up more, Pa taught me and my brothers, Romey and Ervin—our other brother, Ed, died when he was 'bout fourteen—to cook 'moon.' Us folks made putnur everthin' we needed to live. We thought we might as well make our own whiskey, too. So we did. Good stuff it was, too. We was always careful to do it right or a person could poison one's self. Ours was as good a moon as ever was cooked.

"Later on, Romey lived on a island jist south of what's called Mosiman's Slough upriver toward Alma. This was before the government built the locks and dams. Was a rock road over to Romey's place. Many a person went acrosst there to get a little moon from Romey. Once the dams was in, Romey hada move out and his rock road was flooded over. Nowadays, folks think that place is some old wing dam or somethin'. Folks are a fishin' there all the time on topa Romey's road."

The old man continued: "Still cook moon, only for myself though. Never sold a drop in my life. Never will either. Like everthin' else I ever done, it's jist a way to save a nickel or two, to get by the best way I know how. Made many a gallon of wine, too, we did. Blackberry, grape, elderberry, dandelion—you name it, I made it.

"One thing I never could make, never knew anybody who could either, is Copenhagen snuff. Sometimes wish I didn't use it. Makes me beholden to others. Course they say every man outta have one good vice. Notice you use that there snuff, too, don't you?"

I nodded and said, "First thing I'd have to wonder is there such a thing as a good vice? Second thing is you've made everything under the sun, from boats to tools to whiskey, even your own house. If somebody was to ask me, 'What do Ott and Ann know about a self-sufficient lifestyle?' I'd have to answer the list would be a whole lot shorter if one asked what they didn't know. So what stopped you when it came to snuff?"

Ott was slow to answer. He was in a gleeful mood. I could tell by the twinkle in his azure blue eyes and his smile that sent deeply furrowed crow's feet all the way back to his ears.

"Wall, you better know that I thought on it more than once," he said. "Trouble was the recipe I come up with. I figured if I took some fresh horse apples, dried 'em good and proper, then ground 'em up nice and fine, and added a certain amount a molasses or syrup, I might come close to what I needed. Even mentioned it to a few folks who used snuff. Problem was I never could get nobody to do the first taste test of my recipe. I'll mix 'er up if you wanna try it for taste, you young pup."

Starting at his flannel shirt collar, Ott's neck and then his entire head flushed beet red. His shoulders shook, his chest heaved, and finally his entire body erupted in convulsive waves of foghorn-volume baritone laughter.

I calmly sipped from my coffee cup and left things the way they were. The old adage about asking a foolish question ran through my mind as the old man tried to regain his composure.

On an early spring day shortly after ice out, Ott and I were traveling downstream by boat from his place at the north end of Buffalo City. It was one of those days when, for the first time since mid-October, the sun actually seemed to warm one's bones. As usual, Ott was rowing and I was riding on the bow, more or less for ballast, I guess. Ott thought we outta take a look around after the ice went out.

Soon after we passed the Buffalo City resort, Ott quit rowing, placed his oars carefully in the boat, and stared off in his "'cross the river and back in time" gaze. I knew a story was forthcoming. When inspired by longtime surroundings such as these, his stories were truly golden nuggets of the past. A flock of red-winged blackbirds flew high overhead, talking back and forth as the old-timer began:

"Back in the old days, Buffalo City was nothin' more than a flat spot on the bank along Belvidere Slough. First folks here thought the main channel ran against the bank. Sorry, Sarah! That weren't the case! The true channel ran close to the opposite bluffs in Minnesota. Once the spring flood was over, the steamboats couldn't get to Buffalo City no how. Too many islands and shallow water all across the river bottoms to Minnesota. We jist had this one deep slough along our bank. Trouble was it petered out 'fore the steamboats could get into it from the main channel. Oh, what in Sam Hill!" Ott noticed we were drifting beyond the area he was talking about.

"Either I gotta quit talkin', or we gotta quit driftin'," he muttered. Thirty powerful oar strokes later, we were beached on a long, narrow, grassy island sporting numerous clumps of small willows.

When we landed, a large beaver slipped into the water upstream, then slapped its tail with gusto to announce its displeasure at being disturbed during a meal of soft, young willow bark. Ott said, "Sorry 'bout that, old beaver. He can't eat, but now we kin talk." He resumed his story:

"Wall, all them islands 'tween here and Minnesota was covered with marsh grass them days, and putner everbody in Buffalo City had a cow or two. So ever' mornin', folks would get their cows down to the riverbank 'bout the same time, right close where the resort is sittin' now. And ever' day, some of us kids took turns bein' cattle watchers. The old folks'd drive them cattle into the water deep enough to make 'em swim. Then a few of us kids'd get in a boat and follow them cattle 'cross the Buffalo City slough. Was nothin' but horns, heads, and cattle backs going 'cross ahead of us. Them cattle'd crawl out on the first grass island they came to and start eatin'. And we'd watch 'em so's they didn't stray off too far. Kept count of how many there was. Kept on that way, one island to another, all day long.

"Wall, you could figure out what us kids done while them cattle was eatin'. We was a fishin' and wadin' and diggin' up clams with our toes and spearin' bullfrogs and layin' in the shade of the cottonwoods and playin' and swimmin'. Was a three-ring circus with no tent."

The old man laughed and shook his head. "Some of the best days of my life was spent cattle watchin'. Come evenin', we'd herd the whole bunch back across the river bottoms to home. The old folks'd be waitin' on the riverbank. Funny thing it was. Soon as them cattle crawled up the bank, they each started for their own barn. Wern't much sortin' to be done. The sortin' was more about us kids. Who was tendin' the cattle today and who'd be tendin 'em tomorrow. See, it was such a fun job, we all wanted to do it ever' day. Sometimes us kids'd get to squabblin' and fightin' so bad, till one of the old folks'd holler, 'Here now' and point down along the riverbank, 'I kin see from here there's three or four nice green willows'd make dandy switches. Reckon if I went and cut 'em and used 'em among you, it might help you kids to 'member who's rightful turn it is to watch cattle tomorrow and maybe a long ways past that, too!'" Ott recollected, "That pretty much put things in order."

The old river rat stood up with a groan, stretched out his arms, twisted his neck around, and sat back down on his rowing seat. "Used to make meadow hay out here, too, in dry years. Hauled it back for the cattle's winter feed."

He reached for his worn old oars. As we headed back upriver, my mind filled with images of free-grazing cattle on high-banked grassy islands, ragtag kids with suntanned toes, handmade wooden rowboats, and, in the far distance, the ghostly mirage of an ancient steamboat.

On a cold, gray-skied day, when the winter wind howled its way down the Big River valley, I sought comfort and conversation in Ott and Ann's kitchen. With a coffee cup in one hand and one of Ann's homemade cookies in the other, I gathered the courage to ask the question I had always wondered about. "Say, I don't mean to be nosey, but how come your kids, Kathy and Dick, go by the last name of Brommerich?"

"Wall, I think that's 'bout as nosey as you kin get!" Ott's voice boomed off the kitchen walls as he grinned.

Although accustomed to such outbursts, Ann did not, however, find this one to suit her fancy. She gave Ott a steely look, then said, "Oh, he's so fulla hot air, he just might float off one of these days!"

Ann ran her work-worn fingers through her beautiful snow-white hair, as if to clear her mind and to bring forth important memories. She folded her hands in her aproned lap and began, "You see, Kenny, in the late forties, my sister Frances fell on hard times. She struggled hard as she could movin' from place to place. Finally, right about Christmastime in 1947, she come to our place and asked if me and Ottmar would take care of her kids for a while, 'cause she was gonna start a new life in South Dakota. We had no kids of our own and had plenty to eat and room enough for 'em, so we says sure, we'll take good care of 'em for you. Frances left Kathy here; she was only six weeks old. And she left Dick with us; he was eight at the time. It took a little gettin' used to on all our parts, I guess. My sister Frances never did get back here, so we had us a son and a daughter to raise up. I always figured they was the best Christmas present we ever got."

Ott piped up from his corner chair, "Damn well katootin' they was, Ann!" He wiped his eyes with the back of a massive hand and looked out at the river.

Ann smiled gently as she gazed at her coffee cup. "Oh, it was so much fun havin' them two kids around. Everthin' about our lives just seemed to brighten up putnur overnight. Wasn't long and we was a family. Don't know where the next years all went to, though. Went by so fast, it seems. Don't it seem that way to you, Ottmar?"

The old man lurched slightly in his chair as if startled back from some far-off thought of times or places or dreams.

"Yup," he answered. "It all went by so fast. First thing we knew, Dick went all the way through the high school. Never got that far myself, ya know. We was real proud of 'im. Then he joined up with the Marine Corps. Tough bunch they are, kinda like us river rats." He chuckled. "One day, we find out Dick's marryin' up with 'nother Marine name of Chinney, who's an Ojibway Indian from northern Michigan. We was real proud again, 'cause me and Ann grew up with a lotta Indian friends, and they's mighty good people. Anyhow, Dick put in some more years with them Marines, and then in 1964, him and Chinney come home here and built 'em a house downriver from us a little. I was glad."

Ann nodded her head sideways at Ott. "Oh, how I wish he would call his daughter-in-law by her right name for a change. Her name's Virginia. We call her Ginny. All he's ever called her is Chinney!"

Now Ott's dander was up. "Wall, what's the difference how I say her name? I call 'er a damn good woman. Does that suit ya?"

Ann took up the other half of their children's history. "Kathy went through the high school, too, and then even a while in a college. We was real proud of that. Nobody way back in our family ever went to a college. She got to work in offices after that. Some way she happened to get out in the hill country to the little village of Waumandee. Ain't that close to where you was raised up, Kenny?"

"Yup, sure is, Ann," I answered.

"Anyways, she met up with this young guy name of Orlin Brommer. The two of 'em hit it off good right away. Smart young feller he was. Went through full college years, he did. Got to be a schoolteacher. Now he delivers mail out in the country. Kathy and Orlin got married in 1967."

"Judas Priest, I'll never forget that year," Ott broke in. "He's been eatin' me outta house and home ever since! Putnur ever day he'll come bargin' in here like he owns the place. Heads right for the fridge and pours himself the biggest glass of milk he kin find. And I'll say, 'That's the way. That's it, Orlin, we got plenty milk. Why don't ya help yourself to some cookies, while you're at it.' Sure as all Billy Buck he will, but that ain't 'nough to suit him. See, Kenny, there's two cookie chars on the counter over there. Both look the same, 'cept for the covers. Ann puts regular cookies in one and puts my favorite cookies in the other one, what's got the pitcher of a duck on the cover. Orlin's mean 'nough to switch them covers, so when I go to get me a cookie, I'm inta the wrong char. He does it on purpose, claims he gets mixed up, but I know better! That ain't the worst of it. Then he'll bring a couple of hands full of cookies, mostly my favorite ones, and his glass of milk over to the table and lick up the whole shebang like he ain't ate in a week, right ahead a me. That's what really pinches me where the sun don't shine!"

Ann winked at me, and I returned the gesture. Everyone who knew Ott understood that beneath his rough-and-tumble exterior beat a soft, kind, and loving heart. He loved his family and his ongoing cookie jar battle with Orlin.

Whenever I fell behind in processing my trap line catch, I would ask for Ott's help. When it came to skinning, fleshing, stretching, and general all-around handling of furs, Ott was a master. Even into his early eighties, his massive knife-scarred hands moved smoothly, easily, and with precision upon a pelt. Beaver, mink, muskrat, raccoon, fox, and skunk were all treated with respect and the sense of a job well done.

A river rat was a subsistence killer of wild things. Never was anything killed just to watch it die, for sport as they say. "*Nothing wasted, everything used*" was their motto. When a dogfish was caught, it was generally not eaten; however, small pieces were used to catch catfish for the table. Ducks and geese were shot to eat, and their downy feathers used to stuff pillows. Beaver, muskrat, and raccoon were roasted. Skunk fat was rendered into the purest, whitest lard you ever did see. Deer were made into summer sausage, chops, steaks, hamburger, roasts, and cook sausage, and the hide was either tanned or sold. Fish of all kinds were pan-fried, smoked over green hickory, or pickled in glass jars. Turtles became stew or soup. Any part of a critter or fish that could not be used was placed somewhere so that other wild things—eagles, hawks, owls, possums—could make use of it. The death of one meant life for another. The Circle of Life continued unbroken.

One late summer evening as dusk fell upon the Big River, I sat beside Ott on his dock under the giant weeping willow tree. He turned to me. "Them doctors say I got me a cancer."

Stunned, I said nothing.

He went on. "Ain't felt good lately. Reckon I won't be around come spring. Eighty-six years old now. Never thought this old rat'd live this long. You know somethin', you young pup, somethin's gotta use you up. It's a genuine fact."

He extended his arm toward me. His huge hand covered mine; the viselike grip was gone. This time it felt like a caress.

Looking back on the river rat people and the times and places in which they lived, there were certain attributes each possessed: the tenacity of a bulldog, the stubbornness of a mule, and, when the circumstances dictated it, the disposition of a Tasmanian devil.

Their way of life was unknown to the vast majority of American people.

I followed in the footsteps of most, traveled alongside of some, and hope for the future of others to come.

It is a good life to lead.

2. Uncle Whimpy

The wild prairie grasses hung limp. There wasn't a hint of a breeze. Heat rose from the ground and seared my nostrils. Sweat rolled from under my battered felt hat and trickled down my cheeks.

The sudden *thump, thump, thump* of a walking stick pounding the earth turned my attention a hundred feet downhill. I was standing on a goat prairie in the Mississippi River hill country. My eyes focused on the red bandana being wiped across the nut-brown, hairless head below me.

"Hey, Whimpy, did you get one?" I asked in as quiet a voice as I could and still have him hear me.

When hunting rattlesnakes, hollering was not considered correct procedure. Whimpy and all the other old-time snakers hated it when somebody hollered during a goat prairie snake hunt.

"Yup, pretty good-sized one, too. But that's the last one for me today. Too damn hot for an old man like me to crawl around on these blasted hills. I'm headin' for the truck right now."

"Hold up a minute. I'm coming, too." I picked my way down the steep limestone- and sandstone-studded grassy goat prairie. Whimpy leaned on his walking stick, watching my progress. One of the cardinal rules in avoiding being a snake-bit snaker was to never, ever step over anything that you could not look under, such as downed trees, rock ledges, or large tufts of grass.

When I got down to Whimpy, he turned and I followed him down the hill through five hundred yards of tangled woods to my old car.

We took a jug of water from an ice cooler, and both of us sprawled out in the grass beneath the spreading limbs of a big bur oak. Between pulls on the water jug, Whimpy allowed as how "there ain't no place hotter than a goat prairie on a late August day."

He added, "Ain't it funny how in the wintertime, when it's twenty below zero, the wind'll be a howling along at forty miles an hour out of the north—freeze a man stiff right in his tracks. But now, when it's ninety in the shade and there ain't no shade, there ain't enough wind to make a leaf shiver."

"Yup, Uncle Whimpy, it's the darnedest thing and it sure is true." I nodded.

"You know, Kenny, I ain't really your uncle. My pa and your grampa were brothers. I guess that'd make us second cousins."

"I know you ain't my true uncle, but hey, I'm only twenty-one years old and you're thirty-some years older, so it seems better and more right to call you uncle. Anyhow, you feel like an uncle to me."

His hoarse, gravely voice broke into a laugh as he shook his head. "My right name is Wilmer Salwey, but lots of folks call me Whimpy. It's just a nickname. Lots of people got nicknames here along the river. So you just call me anything you want, only not late for dinner." His deep voice rattled with laughter again.

We took our day's catch from our overall pockets. I produced two medium-sized rattles. Whimpy laid two medium and two large sets of rattles in the grass next to mine.

These were the days of bounty hunting. The six snake rattles we had taken would net us thirty dollars: five dollars apiece. Six more dead timber rattlesnakes. Six less rattlesnakes to be found in a farmer's hayfield or grain shock or cattle pasture or in somebody's backyard or porch or garage.

It seemed like a good thing at the time. There was also a bounty of five dollars apiece on red fox, twenty-five cents apiece on pocket gopher, and five cents apiece on striped gopher. For a time, there was a bounty of one dollar each for unborn rattlesnakes as well. The bounty money was collected at the county courthouse or at country stores and taverns all along the Big River. It was a way for some river rats to supplement their income. Rarely were they turned away when they asked private landowners for permission to hunt rattlesnakes.

Whimpy and I lay back in the shady grass and savored the cool drinking water and the restfulness of white, puffy clouds drifting overhead.

After a while, I sat up and took a three-fingered dip of Copenhagen snuff. Whimpy took out the fixings for one of his legendary handmade cigarettes. First, he carefully laid a small package of cigarette papers on his leg. Then he picked out one of the three-inch-square papers and slightly creased it in the middle. This he held between the thumb and forefinger of his left hand. With his right hand, he fished out a can of Prince Albert tobacco from the bib pocket of his overalls, flipped the lid open, and shook just the right amount of tobacco into the cigarette paper. Next, he performed a feat that only time, patience, and practice could produce. In one deft motion of the fingers, he rolled a round, fully packed cigarette. It was a fine thing to behold. A work of art. However, from here on in, the whole process generally slid downhill.

Now it was time to give the perfectly rolled cigarette a quick lick of his tongue to hold it together. Uncle Whimpy was as toothless as a newborn baby. He had a set of what he called false plates. However, the plates were most times at home, soaking in a glass of water. Therefore, when he went to lick the cigarette, he was unable to control the amount of saliva he applied. It was amazing. The cigarette entered his mouth on one side, held horizontally—so round, so fully packed—then crossed his tongue, where he slathered it with saliva, and came out the other side of his mouth looking as if it had been dropped in a mud puddle. At first glance, this would not seem like a major problem. However, the next step, that of lighting the thing on fire and keeping it burning, could prove to be the next thing to impossible.

At times, under the right conditions, when Uncle Whimpy did not feel an urgent need for nicotine, he would take the time to dry the sodden thing on the sunlit hood of the car or perhaps balance it on his leg until it was dry. At other times, when he felt the need to smoke right now, he was not totally unprepared. As a rule, he carried at least fifty old-time wooden stick matches wrapped in waxed paper and bound with a strong rubber band to hold the lighting packet together.

Today was a "smoke now" day. Through much practice, Whimpy had perfected another unusual practice: that of striking a stick match to fire on his bib overall buttons, which were made of metal. This he promptly did and held it to the end of the cigarette. A smudgelike smoke began to rise; however, none of it reached his mouth. The match burned out. He tried another one. And then one more. Finally, he was able to draw smoke through the twisted, misshapen, soggy, sorry excuse for a cigarette.

He often joked about all the money he saved by not wearing his store-bought teeth, 'cause it took him forever to smoke a cigarette.

We lay back in the grass. For the next couple of hours, it was story time about snake-hunting and the people who practiced this strange summertime way of life. Whimpy mentioned how he had been watching me over the past summer or two and how he was generally pleased with what he'd been seeing.

"You're going to make the grade as a full-fledged snaker, my boy. It don't matter how many you get. It's how careful you are that counts. It ain't like huntin' squirrels, you know. A mistake there ain't gonna hurt you none except in the fryin' pan. These here critters we're after can cause you some real bad damage."

He rolled up the right arm of his long-sleeved cotton shirt. On his bare forearm, two white, round scars the size of dimes stared back at me. They lay about an inch apart.

He began: "'Bout thirty years ago, my brother Ed and I were a huntin' snakes on a goat prairie up along the Beef River Valley. It was a day like today, hotter than the mill tails of hell. I killed a medium-sized rattler in knee-high grass. Went and reached down and grabbed that snake by the tail, put my foot on its head, and was about to cut the rattles off when, *kathump*, something hit my arm. Looked at my arm and there was two holes in it. They was a bleedin' some and there was a little white-colored juice seepin' out of them holes. I took my stick and swept it through the grass, and sure enough, one started to rattle in there. That bugger never made a sound the first time around. I done killed it and cut the rattles off and went and found my brother Ed. I says, 'I been snake-bit, Ed.' He set off a tirade about how could I be so damn dumb and foolish and careless. Him bein' older than me, he was always like that, you know.

"He thought we outta get started down the hill for the car and then to Mondovi for the doctor. He grumbled all the way down the hill and all the way drivin' for the doctor. I never knew whether he was scared for my safety or mad 'cause I ruined a good day of snake-huntin'. Well, old Doc Sharp took a look at the bite at his house and took and cut an X across the two holes, then he put a rubber suction cup over the whole works and pumped on the cup. When he drew it away, there weren't a whole lot of white juice in it, so he says to me, 'Whimpy, that snake bit something else before it got ahold of you. So you didn't get a full dose of venom, the way it looks to me. I'd advise you to go on home and lay down real quiet for a day or two, get some ice and pack it in towels around your arm, and take some aspirin and maybe a shot of whiskey every now and then.'"

Whimpy continued: "Well, I didn't have no money on me, so Brother Ed had to pay old Doc the five dollars we owed him. I guess it was the five dollars *I* owed old Doc. That added a little more fuel to the fire that was already burnin' under Brother Ed's butt. I could see it on him, and I knew I wouldn't hear the end of this day's story for the rest of my life."

Uncle Whimpy abruptly stopped his storytelling/teaching session to fashion another cigarette. Twenty minutes later, after using up six stick matches and a fair amount of patience, he finally had his tobacco creation smoking to his liking.

He began again: "Ed took me home, you know, down along Catfish Slough, where I lived with Ma and my twin sister, Wilma. When Ma seen me come through the door with my shirt off and my right arm startin' to swell up pretty good, she asked what in the world happened.

"Ed piped up. 'The damn fool got himself snake-bit on account of being careless and foolish. Had to drive him clean up to Mondovi. Old Doc Sharp said to put this ice we got here around his arm for a while and to keep him quiet. I'm going back up on the hills for a while.'

"Ma and Wilma took good care of me for a few days. My arm swelled up to the size of a stovepipe and it turned every color in a rainbow and then some. All the skin peeled off it. Took me a while to get to use it right again.

"When I tell you to be careful huntin' snakes, you listen, 'cause I know what happens when you ain't. Most times, a bite ain't gonna kill a healthy adult person. Even so, it ain't no Sunday School picnic to get bit."

He held his bare forearm out for me to look at again. The two round, white fang marks drove his lesson home.

"Another thing that kin be dangerous when you're huntin' snakes is bees. Yellow jackets like to nest in the ground. There you are, pokin' your stick under them rock ledges, feelin' for snakes. All of a sudden, a swarm of yellow jackets come out from under there. They ain't happy campers. They are little, quick buggers, and once they get an idea of what's bothering 'em, they'll get onto you and they'll stay on you as long as they kin. It would be nice to just up and run away from 'em as fast as you could. However, there just could be another problem waitin' for you as you run down the hill. Just could happen that you'd run over the top of a snake. You'd end up not only bee-stung in forty different places but snake-bit at the same time. So if them bees ever get on you, try the best you can to watch where you're running to, okay?"

I nodded. "Okay, Uncle Whimpy, I will."

For another hour or so, he and I discussed all the old-time snakers that we knew. Every little river town harbored some.

In Winona, Minnesota, there was Bobby Fort, who most times caught his snakes alive with his bare hands. Bobby would save up his snakes and sell them in batches to folks who would extract the venom for snakebite medicine.

In later years, Bobby became a fur buyer. I once took some furs to Bobby's house to sell. He welcomed me and told me to sit down in a stuffed chair in the living room. I no more than sat down when I heard an all-too-familiar buzzing rattle beneath me. There was no doubt in my mind there was a rattlesnake under my chair. I held my feet real quiet.

Bobby looked over at me. "Don't you worry none, Kenny. He's in a gunnysack. Thought you might get a kick outta that." He roared with laughter.

The Neimier family also did a great deal of snake-hunting in the Winona area. They usually hunted for bounty.

In the Whitewater Valley around Elba, Minnesota, lived the most famous of all snakers: William "Black Bill" Vensel. He caught his snakes alive and kept them in a wire pen at his cabin on the north branch of the Whitewater River. Black Bill was a true showman and snake-handler. He would often put on live rattlesnake shows for Scout groups and tourists. Nevertheless, he was bitten a number of times. After his death, it was said that he died of an enlarged heart, due to the many snake bites that he suffered. True or not, it remains part of the legend of Black Bill.

Near Fountain City and Eagle Valley, it was a man named Kenny Baertch who caught snakes alive and killed them for bounty as well. In the Waumandee and Cream area, Pete, Elmer, and Oscar Blank all did some snaking from time to time.

It was, however, in the river towns of Alma and Nelson, Wisconsin, where the most snakers lived. Joe Hanson, Bill Moore, Ed Salwey, "Rattlesnake" Andy Jimison, and Wilmer "Whimpy" Salwey all lived there, along with a few youngsters like Donny Ganz Senior and me, who tagged along with the old-timers.

Donny Ganz Senior went to Oklahoma every year to participate in the state's Rattlesnake Roundup until just recently, when his health began to fail. Donny, like me, has spent a great deal of time around snakes and has learned to love and respect them for what they are: a beautiful and necessary part of the great Circle of Life. Donny and I only live a couple of miles from each other, so we often have a chance to visit back and forth about the old days of snaking and the old-timers we knew. And how the timber rattlesnake is now protected and also the swamp rattlesnake and rightly so they should be. The goat prairies have all but disappeared, 'cause there's no burning done on the hills anymore to keep the trees from covering up the open prairies.

As for the swamp rattlesnake, it, too, is losing its habitat. The seasonally flooded hardwood swamps are shrinking. However, there is hope. The Department of Natural Resources is trying as best it can to restore and improve the homes of these elusive, wonderful critters.

The bounty system is now long gone for all critters in Wisconsin. I think that's a good thing. It never seemed to work as intended anyway.

Uncle Whimpy and I were still mulling over snakes and such when it finally dawned on both of us that the sun had rolled around to suppertime position.

Whimpy was never in a hurry, probably 'cause he was a lifelong confirmed bachelor and had no one to answer to at a certain time or place. It was, however, summertime and snake-hunting was not the only thing we did this time of year. There were set lines for catfish to put out before dark.

At this time in his life, Whimpy did not drive a car, so I drove him home. Home to him was a small, somewhat ramshackle cross between a cabin and a cottage, which he shared with his mother, a small, thin, wiry woman who was in her late seventies and rarely spoke a word of English. His twin sister, Wilma, also lived there. Highway 35 was on the east side of their home, about fifty yards away. The Burlington Northern Railroad ran seventy-five yards to the west. Most of the south end of the Nelson Bottoms flowed into Catfish Slough, just across the railroad tracks from Uncle Whimpy's house.

On the way there, he said, "Ma and Wilma will have the set lines baited up and ready to go when I get there. You know, Kenny, I made all new lines this winter. Good strong main lines, got two-foot staging lines on brass swivels at each end, sharp number 2 stainless-steel hooks. Put floats on some, lead weights on others, and put a couple of cork floats, then a couple of lead weights, then more floats, and so on the rest for jump lines, so a guy can catch 'em whether they're bitin' on the top or the bottom. Been usin' cut-up dogfish lately. Doin' pretty good, too. The other morning, we had a thirty-two-pound mudcat. He'd swallowed a foot-long channel cat. Got 'em both at the same time. The best bait for mudcats is small- to medium-sized sunfish. Trouble is, it's illegal."

Whimpy paused. "Say, did I ever tell you about the time Ma and I was puttin' out set lines and that big storm come up?"

Did he ever tell me? The question was more like how many times. However, one did not say such things to old-timers. "Maybe you did," I said, "but I'd still like to hear it again."

He launched into it full bore. "Well, it was one of them late August days, a lot like today. Hot, sticky, not a leaf movin'. You could sweat just thinkin' about doin' something. An hour or so before dark, Ma and me rowed out into Catfish Slough in my old sixteen-foot wooden boat. We had four set line boxes aboard, a hundred hooks to the box. You know you put 'em out just before dark, so the turtles and little fish don't eat all the bait off before the big catfish get to it." He looked at me.

I nodded. "Yup, that's for sure."

"Well, we set some lines in the deep water. Ma always rows the boat while I feed the lines out of the boxes, you know. Then we went to the west and set the other lines in shallow water. All of a sudden, a big black cloud comes a rollin' in over the Minnesota hills. Thunder and lightning is a crashin' all around. The wind starts to blow and howl. Ma can't handle the oars no more, on account of the waves being so high and roiley, so I takes a hold of them oars and told Ma to get down low in the boat. Now I'm lendin' my back to them oars just as hard as I can, and them waves are a poundin' and splashin', and Ma's croutchin' in the bottom of that boat. It didn't look good for us about then, and sure enough, they got worse as it went along. We was about three-quarters of the way across Catfish Slough when I just couldn't keep that boat headed straight anymore. It turned sideways and over we went, all in one motion. Quicker than the flick of a cat's tail, we was in the water. I woulda liked to grab hold of the boat, but I had to find Ma, 'cause she can't swim a stroke, you know. Lived around water all her life and can't swim." He looked over at me to see if I was paying attention.

"Yup, I ain't a great swimmer myself," I said. "Lots of river folks are that way. Nowadays, they even got swimming pools in river towns. Strange, don't you think?"

Uncle Whimpy cleared his throat. "Anyhow, there we were in the water, me lookin' where Ma was and the boat floatin' away in a big hurry. I saw her bobbin' in the waves about ten feet away, so I swam over to her and rolled her on her back. I told her to try to rest herself and took her around the neck and under one arm with my right hand and started to swim for shore, towing her along behind me. For luck was the waves was mostly headed in that direction.

"All of a sudden, I hear her a singin' and laughin'. I leaned over on my side for a second or two, and I saw that the wind was a blowin' up under that big long dress she always wore. It was billowing up in the air and acted purty near like a sail. She was as light as a feather to pull along. There was some folks fishin' along the bank there, and they'd seen the whole thing happen. When we got in fairly close to the bank, they started to wade out to help us in to safety. Them folks acted awful confounded when they found a little seventy-six-year-old woman layin' in the water a singin' and laughin', and they couldn't understand a word she was sayin'. I thanked them for their efforts and said we was all right. But we sure got some strange looks when we trudged up over the railroad tracks to our house up yonder.

"The next morning, I found the old boat blowed up into a cove about a mile downstream. One oar was missin'. That's all. Could have been a whole lot worse, I guess. Ma still says it was one of the most fun days of her life."

I asked Whimpy how old his mother was now. He said she'd be eighty years old her next birthday. He allowed as how she was one reason he never got married. "You just can't find a woman like that no more nowadays. Ma helps me skin muskrats, clean turtles and fish, helps me stretch beaver, does the laundry and the cookin', works in the garden with me. She allowed an old bull snake to live in our root cellar for years in order to keep the mice population down. He stayed under a raised-up plank in the south corner. Was about five feet long, I'd guess. One day he turned up missin'. Found him up on the road. Some damn fool run him over. Wilma and I and Ma cried over it. Some folks are so scared of snakes they'll run 'em over on purpose. Better mousers than most cats, they are."

Within the next ten years, Uncle Whimpy's twin sister, Wilma, died and his mother's health began to fail as well. A couple of times a week, Whimpy would walk up the road or follow the railroad tracks a mile and a half to the little river town of Nelson, Wisconsin. There he purchased a few grocery staples and, most times, a few beers at the Nelson Hotel and Saloon. On one of these trips to town, he was perched on a barstool and Bob the bartender noticed that Whimpy was nursing his glass of beer and simply was not his usual talkative self. So Bob leaned across the bar and said, "Whimpy, you seem kinda down in the mouth today. Is anything the matter?"

"Is somethin' the matter!" Whimpy boomed. Everybody in the saloon turned to hear what it was.

"Well, Bob, for starters, you know my sister, Wilma, up and died a few years back, and that left Ma and me a good pair of hands short." He looked at Bob, and the bartender nodded his head.

Whimpy went on. "About six months ago, Ma started to keel over every now and then, on account of faintin' spells. We took her to the doctor, and he gave her some pills. Helped her some at first. Then she'd started to keel over more and more. So we took her to the doctor again, and he said Ma belonged in a rest home where she'd have better care. Brother Ed and I talked it over quite a bit. Finally, a couple of days ago we took her and put her into the Pepin Rest Home. So there she is now, ninety years old is all she is and sittin' in a place she don't wanna be."

"Yup, your ma always was tough as shoe leather," Bob said. "Shame to see her go like that, Whimpy."

"That ain't the worst of it, Bob," Whimpy began again. "I guess now I'll have to quit set lining, 'cause Ma ain't with me no more to row the boat."

Bob stared at him for a moment, shook his head, and slowly walked away.

News of that sort travels fast along the river, and the story is still being told and retold to this very day. Most folks agree that Whimpy should have been rowing his boat himself rather than having his poor old mother doing the job. I think, however, there was much more to it than that. She was a true river rat in her own right. She knew as much as or more than he did about where, when, and how to put out set lines. That, coupled with the fact that he truly loved and respected his mother and enjoyed and valued her company, suggests that maybe, just maybe, the story of a woman who rowed a boat for her son almost every day from April through October till she was ninety years old isn't quite as strange as it appears to be at first glance.

Whimpy did quit set lining, and within a year or so, he, too, was living in a rest home in Cochrane, Wisconsin. Often, I would take him along on outdoors adventures.

In the fall, he loved to go duck-hunting in the Whitman Swamp. By that time, he had sold all of his guns, so he used an old single-shot 12 gauge of mine. He never carried more than a handful of shells in his pocket at a time.

"No need to carry a whole sack full of shells, Kenny," he'd say. "You just put up the gun, keep both eyes open, start behind the bird, swing the barrel along with 'em, then a little past 'em, and shoot. It's like usin' a broom. You just kinda sweep 'em outta the sky all in one motion."

Whimpy was a crack shot, despite having what to most people would seem to be a handicap when it came to shooting a gun. When he was a young man, he earned a little extra money in the summertime by working in a local sawmill. One day, they were sawing oak logs with a large circular saw blade and he slipped as the log went into the saw. His right hand hit the blade, taking off his right index finger all the way back to the inside of his thumb.

After that, it became necessary for him to use his middle finger to pull the trigger of a gun. In cold weather, the forefinger of his right-hand glove flopped about, so he would sometimes tape it flat to the back of his hand to keep it out of the way.

However, shoot he could. When he dropped a duck, he took great pleasure in watching my hunting dogs retrieve the birds for him. He would sit on the banks of the sloughs and ponds in his ever-present bib overalls, hip boots rolled to the knee, ragged old canvas hunting coat open, and pet and praise the dogs to no end.

In late fall and early winter, Whimpy went on the trap line with me along the cricks and small rivers in the hill country. We were after mink, muskrats, and raccoons. I drove an old telephone truck in those days, which had a high covered back end and pullout drawers on each side.

I would check the traps and bring the critters back to the truck, where Whimpy would hang them inside to dry. Once they were dry, he would skin them and put the furs in the drawers.

One year, we teamed up with a friend of mine, Ronny Haney, to trap muskrats on Gramma Haney's land in the Milton Bottoms. The three of us had put out a number of traps by canoe in open water and were doing quite well for a week or so. One morning, we came to the swamp after a hard overnight freeze. There was about an inch of clear ice covering the water, so we couldn't use the canoes to check our traps.

Uncle Whimpy stood on the shore and said, "Boys, ain't no use in tryin' to check them traps today. Ice is too thick for a canoe and too thin to walk on. If you go in there walkin' to what traps you can reach, you'll do nothin' but cut holes in your hip boots. That's all you'll do. We got to wait till the ice gets thicker or it warms up and the ice melts. The rats will be okay where they are. They're dead and the water's cold."

Ronny and I looked at Whimpy, then at each other. We pulled up our hip boots and headed into the water, breaking ice as we went.

An hour later, Ronny and I stumbled up the bank with a few rats each in a gunnysack and two pairs of hip boots cut to ribbons as if we'd taken a knife to them at the knees.

Uncle Whimpy was sitting on a stump fixing himself a homemade cigarette. He looked up while we were dumping the water out of our boots. "Well, I guess there goes the profits for today. You boys will be buyin' a couple of pairs of new boots, won't you now?" He chuckled and shook his head.

Throughout the coming years, each season brought its own kind of river rat work to be done. I tried to include Whimpy as much as I could, for I knew in my heart that a little taste of the old ways was the only thing making life bearable for him living in a rest home. Although it had always been in his nature to complain some—hence the nickname "Whimpy"—at the home it was pretty much nonstop. The cooking wasn't worth a damn, the laundry wasn't done right, his roommates weren't playing with a full deck of cards, and the staff wasn't treating him right.

He began changing homes. He went to Alma, then to a boarding house in Cochrane, and back to the Cochrane rest home again.

Every couple of weeks, I'd take him to the rest home at Pepin, Wisconsin, to visit his mother. She died just a little short of her hundredth birthday.

Whimpy said, "Right to the end, Ma talked of the old days along the banks of Catfish Slough and thought she could still row a boat if she'd had the chance to do so."

After the funeral, at her gravesite, Whimpy turned to me and through bleary eyes said, "Kenny, she was a mighty good ma to me." He took a red bandana handkerchief from his bib overall back pocket, blew his nose, and slowly walked away.

The one place where Whimpy was content was out-of-doors. It didn't matter what he was doing as long as it was outside. I believe, however, that trout fishing was his favorite outdoors pursuit. The entire Salwey family were—and still are—avid trout anglers. We fish in Wisconsin, Minnesota, and Iowa streams, cricks, and small rivers for the most part.

Back in those days, the Minnesota trout season opened on the fifteenth of March. One year, my good friend Jim Everson, our local Buffalo County game warden, asked whether we'd have room for his twelve-year-old son, Timmy, to go along with us. I said we sure enough would, so early in the morning on the fifteenth of March, we stopped at Jim and Marge Everson's house to pick Timmy up. When I went in to get him, his dad handed him a nice new fly rod.

The last thing his dad said as we went out the door was, "Timmy, you take good care of that fly rod. It's one of those newfangled graphites. Cost me a pretty penny."

Jim added, "You watch and listen close today and you'll learn a lot from the Salweys."

We loaded young Timmy's gear into the trunk of my beat-up old car, and he crawled into the back seat between my dad, Willard Salwey, and Whimpy Salwey. I drove and my nephew Tim Salwey rode in the passenger seat.

We headed down the road toward Crooked Crick Valley near Reno, Minnesota, seventy-five miles south of us. There was still a foot or more of snow on the ground, so the going was slow. As was usually the case, to pass the time, we began to swap yarns and tell stories. Of those present, Whimpy was far and away the master of such entertainment. Today, there is a popular saying: "That sounds like a stretch to me." I'm here to tell you back then there were a whole lot of hill folk and river rats who could and did "stretch" a genuine fact until it was unrecognizable. As a matter of fact, stretching was practiced until it became an art form to be proud of.

Whimpy started off with a forty-five-minute account of how the white-tailed deer were slaughtered back in the hills years ago. "Why, a bunch of us would line up and down a whole hillside, 'bout fifty yards apart. The slugs in them days didn't carry as far as they do now, you know. Then another bunch of us would circle around a few hills upwind of the first bunch, spread out some, and start walkin' towards 'em. Us that was walkin' would shoot a deer now and then for sure. But, Sonny, the shootin' that went on over there where they was a standing it off was just somethin' awful. You'd a thought there was a war going on over there. By the time we got to where the first bunch was, there was deer layin' all over the place. The snow was red with blood all over them hills. Wasn't it now, Willard?"

I looked in the rearview mirror. Dad's head twitched to one side. This was a telling move. There was no nod of approval, no shake of disagreement. Only the sharp sideways twitch and slight lift of his shoulders, which meant, "Could have been that way, I guess."

Timmy looked quickly back at Whimpy, who was wiping his completely hairless head with a red bandana. "Turn that heater down some, will you, Kenny? Well, Sonny, all the rest of that day we was a guttin' deer and a draggin' deer down the hills. We stacked 'em up like cordwood. Pickup trucks full of 'em. All night long, we was a skinning deer. Never wasted any though. Them was tough times. We ate anything we could lay our hands on and was glad of it. Wasn't we, Willard?"

Dad's voice piped up—no head movements now. "You bet them was tough times. Hope you don't ever have to go through tough times, Timmy." Dad patted Timmy's knee.

Now it was Dad's turn to recall old times and places. "Timmy, I was born and raised in a place called Jahn's Valley, just a little past Cream, Wisconsin, on Highway 88. You turn east into a narrow valley with a crick running down through it."

Both Whimpy and Dad's focus was on Timmy Everson. After all, he was a captive audience seated between the two of them. My nephew Tim and I had heard these stories so many times that either of us could have recounted them word for word.

However, there was something about the two old-timers in the back seat that only time itself could provide. It was not only the words they were saying. It was their lined, wrinkled, weather-beaten faces. Their gnarled, knobby, swollen, and scarred hands demanded the undivided attention of young Timmy Everson.

Dad continued, "When my brother, Ervin, and my sister, Mildred, and I was kids, our dad would send us down to the crick, which ran down the valley through our cow pasture to catch us a bunch of brook trout for supper.

"Now, Timmy, we didn't take nothin' but a couple of metal milk pails with us. No fishin' poles, no worms, no nets, no nothin'. Ain't nobody in their natural mind would think us kids was a goin' fishin'. When we got to the crick, we pretty much knew where the best trout holes were. We'd roll up our pant legs, take off our shoes, and get to buildin' dams outta rocks on the upstream side and the downstream side of that trout hole. Then we'd all three kids wade right into that trout hole. The trout'd got to goin' crazy tryin' to get away from us, but there was no place for 'em to go, 'cause we had both ends of that hole dammed off. Naturally, a certain number of 'em would end up tryin' to get out of the up- or downstream ends of that hole. My sister, Mildred, was, for the most part, the true trout catcher of our family. She had the quickest hands, so she'd go to one of our rock dams and scoop up any trout she could and throw 'em into a pail that had a little water in it to keep 'em alive. Timmy, you should have seen her go to work a throwin' them trout into them pails. She worked at it like a machine, didn't she, Whimpy?"

Dad paused to catch his breath while Whimpy took up the slack. "Yup, you know, Willard, I never seen anybody who had quicker hands than Cousin Mildred did, male or female considered."

This allowed Dad to carry on. "Well, Timmy, my brother, Ervin, and I was a thrashin' around in the deeper water of that trout hole, scaring them trout back and forth. Sister Mildred would grab a few at one end of the hole, throw 'em in the pail, then go to the other end, grab what she could there, and pail 'em as well.

"When she thought we had enough for supper, she'd holler and we'd all crawl out on the bank to rest awhile. Then we'd take turns carryin' them pails of trout up to the house. Our Ma, Anna, would bring out some butcher knives, and we'd sit around for a while cleanin' them trout up for supper.

"We'd feed the innards and heads and tails and such to our farm cats. Boy, would they ever push and shove and carry on over them trout parts. Them cats shouldn't a had to worry, 'cause there was plenty for all of 'em and then some leftover.

"Ma would put a bunch of bacon grease in a great big old cast-iron fryin' pan, and when the grease started to bubble, she'd roll them trout in a bowl full of flour and cornmeal. Then she'd drop 'em into the fryin' pan and salt and pepper 'em as they was fryin'.

"I'm here to tell you, Timmy, there was no better eatin' than them brook trout that we took out of that ice-cold water and a hour or so later my ma fried 'em up to perfection. There was five of us at the table, so we ate up a whole bunch of trout at one meal. That was over sixty years ago, and I can still taste 'em. Mmm, was they ever good."

Whimpy chimed in. "Yup, Willard, all the old-time women knew how to fry up a pretty darn good fish, but your ma could make 'em up so as a person could hardly quit eatin'. Eat yourself sick if you weren't careful. You see, Sonny, back in them days, we had no freezers. When we got a hunger for somethin', we went out and got what we needed. Sometimes in the fall, we'd get wild ducks and mud hens and such by the gunnysacks full. Didn't pay much attention to licenses or limits. It was our bellies we listened to then."

I winked at my nephew, Tim, and he smiled as he slightly shook his head.

Poor Timmy Everson was stuck in the back seat between two old-time yarn-spinners who cared not one whit that he was the game warden's son.

By now, we were in the Crooked Crick Valley. A short time later, I pulled the car to the side of the road near a bridge. I opened the trunk, and we each took our individual trout-fishing gear from it. When we were all ready to head for the crick, I told Timmy to close the trunk. I heard him shut the trunk. As Whimpy, Dad, Nephew Tim, and

I walked along the road, I noticed Timmy was missing. I turned to see where he was. He was still standing by the car, so I went back to find out what was wrong.

"Boy oh boy, I sure went and did it now. I slammed Dad's brand-new graphite fly rod between the trunk and the lid." He held the broken rod out for me to see, as tears welled up in his eyes.

"Dad's gonna be awful mad," he sniffled.

It was any twelve-year-old kid's worst nightmare. He had looked forward to this day for months. His dad had allowed him to use a beautiful, costly new rod, which now lay shattered against the car, and he'd not even had the chance to get a line wet. A fishing trip just doesn't get a whole lot worse than that.

By this time, the rest of our gang had gathered 'round to offer advice and to try to comfort the boy as best they could.

Uncle Whimpy took the first crack at it. "Yup, Sonny, I lost a few good fishing poles to them darned car trunk lids myself. It's no fun, I kin tell you that much, Sonny."

Then it was my dad's turn. "One time, Kenny and I got too lazy to take our poles apart. We was only gonna drive a little ways down the crick, so we rolled down the back-seat window and stuck the poles in there. We only drove a couple hundred feet when, all of a sudden, both our reels started to whine and screech somethin' awful. We'd drove under a low-hangin' tree branch that'd caught a hold of both rod tips, snapped 'em off, and hung onto our fishin' lines, too. By the time I got the car stopped, we had two broken rods and all our fishin' line was stripped off of our reels. You talk about a mess! 'Member that, Kenny?"

"Woooo, do I remember that. Took us an hour or more to untangle everything, and there was deer flies dive-bombing us all the while to boot."

Then I told Timmy that I'd go into his house with him when we got home to help him explain the whole thing to his dad. And how we'd catch some nice trout today for sure. And we'd make sure he brought them through the door, along with his dad's broken pole.

Timmy's face still looked pretty forlorn, until Nephew Tim spoke up. "Timmy, I've got an extra pole along. We'll rig that up so's you kin at least do some fishin' today. Then we'll deal with the broken pole tonight. For now, let's get on down to the crick. Them trout are waitin' for us."

Now a slight smile crossed Timmy's face. And a bigger one appeared when he pulled a nice, fat, sixteen-inch brown trout up onto the snowbank at his feet a short time later.

By midafternoon, we all had our limit of five trout, each packed in a cooler between layers of roadside snow.

The ride home was much quieter. The two old-timers in the back seat mostly took turns snoring, due to their years lived and the fact that they had spent the day wading through knee-deep snow and breathing cold, crisp air.

Young Timmy spent the ride in deep, thoughtful silence, undoubtedly rehearsing his entrance through his parents' front door and beyond.

Nephew Tim and I, meanwhile, traded observations on the condition of the crick, how the holes had changed, what trout lived where, and where could we catch a big one next time. Such is the talk of all dyed-in-the-wool trout anglers.

Once at home, I went into the house with Timmy. His parents' eyes widened at the beautiful trout he had caught. His father's eyes also widened when he saw the condition of his new graphite fly rod. The only thing he said was, "What was the last thing I told you when you left this morning concerning my rod, Timmy?"

A week or so later, I ran into Jim Everson at the local gas station. He said, "Kenny, thank you so very much for taking Timmy along trout fishing. He got an education about trout fishing, about taking care of gear, and, best of all, about old-timers. As soon as you and your family left our house that night, Timmy went over the day's events with his mom and me—how he so enjoyed being with you folks and fishing for trout and eating your homemade sausage for lunch and how sorry he was about breaking my rod. However, then he says, 'You should have heard some of the stories they told me about killing pickup loads full of deer and catching pails full of trout and shooting gunnysacks full of ducks. I think they might have been pulling my leg a little bit, don't you, Dad?' I was so proud of him that night. I said, 'Yes, Timmy, I think they were, but that's part of the fun of being around old-timers, ain't it?'"

On another trout-fishing trip, I was driving, Nephew Tim was in the passenger seat, and Bob Bitzan and Uncle Whimpy were in the back seat. If there were more than two people on such trips, Uncle Whimpy was sure to ride in the back, because of a most peculiar habit of his.

If he was in the front seat, he would, at certain unpredictable times, suddenly slam his fist down on the dash and point a finger to the side of the road—with no explanation whatsoever as to what he was slamming and pointing about.

Even to those of us who knew Whimpy's ways, it caused a certain amount of reaction: a quickened heartbeat, a jerk of the steering wheel, eyes invariably leaving the road in a quick search for danger.

It was, however, quite another matter for a driver who had the misfortune of having Whimpy riding in the front seat for the very first time. Yes, we would warn them beforehand. However, Whimpy's "slam/point" action was the sort of thing one was never really prepared for. Within a second or two of its occurrence, the brakes were locked up and the driver fought to bring the vehicle under control, especially on the gravel back roads of crick country. The driver frantically looked for a car coming out of a driveway or a side road. Or for a dog or a cat crossing the road beneath their wheels. Or perhaps a deer or a cow coming up out of the roadside ditch any second. However, it was difficult to see because of the cloud of dust caused by the skidding wheels.

Finally, wiping the cold sweat from his brow, the driver would ask Whimpy what he had seen.

At times, Whimpy would answer, "Nice-lookin' barn back there, wasn't it?" Or, "Did you see the size of that Angus bull? I never seen one so big in my natural life." At other times, he would stare straight ahead in complete silence, working his lips back and forth.

So Whimpy generally rode in the back seat in regard for the safety of all aboard.

It was a clear, hot day in mid-July. By early afternoon, we were thirsty and tired, so we stopped at a saloon in a small southeastern Minnesota town to get ourselves a cold drink.

There were perhaps twenty people in the place, mostly retired farmers playing cards and talking over old times and the crops and weather.

Now, no one remained a stranger to Whimpy very long. He would talk to anybody, anytime, about anything, and in any place you could imagine.

In a short while, he stood up, fished a hand-sized metal object from his bib overall pocket, and announced to all within earshot, "With this here little gadget, I not only kin but will show you how to light a cigarette on fire using only the sun to do it. And I'm willing to bet the best drink in the house to prove it's so. Anybody wants to see it done, just follow me."

He headed for the door with about ten people behind him, plus his three fishing pals.

There in the middle of the Main Street sidewalk, Uncle Whimpy held court. Not trusting one of his saliva-slathered homemade cigarettes, he borrowed one from an onlooker and held it up for all to see. "This is a genuine factory-made cigarette, right, folks?" His "Gravel Gerty" voice boomed out for all to hear.

He held up his metal gadget. "This here round part is a mirror on a hinge. Below it here is these two prongs." He placed the cigarette between the prongs and began a series of moves. He looked up at the sun, shielding his eyes with his hand like an Indian surveying the landscape. Then he held the gadget up toward the sun and adjusted the mirror to catch the sun's rays. This he did three or more times, until he was satisfied with the angle.

By this time, half of the people who happened to pass by on the sidewalk had joined the crowd around Whimpy.

At last, a tiny wisp of smoke appeared at one end of the cigarette. Whimpy put his lips to the other end and drew a long slow breath. More smoke appeared, and finally he took the cigarette from the gadget, puffed hard on it a few times, and blew several smoke rings into the hot July air.

A cheer went up from the crowd. They clapped their hands as Whimpy took a long, slow bow, then wiped his hairless head with his ever-present red bandana. He slowly walked back into the saloon, followed by a good number of the onlookers.

Once inside, he began to cash in on the bet he had made earlier. The onlookers provided him with the best drink in the house—and, as is said in advertisements, much, much more. In a short while, Whimpy had hit his full stride as a yarn-spinner. And he knew half the folks in the saloon by their first names, and everyone in there knew his.

Soon there were cries of "Whimpy, bring that cigarette-lightin' gadget over here and show us how it works, will you, buddy?" From the far corner came, "Hey, Whimpy, come on over here. I want these guys to meet a real old-time river rat from over on the Mississippi." In the center of the crowd, someone hollered, "Listen up here, if you wanna hear something that'll make you shiver. Whimpy, tell us again how you got rattlesnake-bit over in them Wisconsin hills."

Then someone began to act as a carnival barker would, for everyone knew by now that Whimpy was a good sport and game for just about anything. The barker shouted, "Come, gather 'round him. He's a river rat. He walks, he talks, he crawls on his belly like a reptile. One thin dime is all it costs. Touch him, folks. He won't bite—much!"

Whimpy roared with laughter along with the crowd.

After several renditions of "For He's a Jolly Good Fellow" had been sung, we finally extracted Whimpy from the saloon, helped him down the front steps, and poured him into the back seat of my old car.

During the first half hour of our ride home, there was a great deal of talk and laughter. The rest of the way home, there was a great deal of snoring.

Another eventful trout-fishing trip took us to northeastern Iowa. It took over one hundred miles to get there, and during most of the ride, from his usual seat in the back, Whimpy complained about the fact that his "piles" were acting up again. Now, it should be understood that the word "hemorrhoid" did not appear in the vocabulary of hill folk or river rats at that time. This physical problem was simply known as a case of the piles and, as a matter of fact, is still known as such to this very day by most folks in our area.

As we passed through a small town, Whimpy's raspy voice suddenly blurted out, "There's a drugstore. Pull over. I gotta get me some medication right now!"

We pulled up to the drugstore. To stretch our legs a bit, Nephew Tim and I went inside with Whimpy.

Tim and I picked up a couple of items that were needed at home and went to the cash register counter, which was tended by a blue-gray-haired, well-manicured elderly lady wearing a pair of glasses around her neck on a strap. She took our money and thanked us kindly.

Whimpy came to the counter next, set a large jar of Vicks VapoRub down, and reached for his wallet. As an afterthought, he said, "I s'pose you think I want this stuff on account of I got me a cold or such."

Without waiting for an answer, he went on, "Well, it's the best stuff there is for that purpose. But I'll tell ya somethin' else it's good for, missus. You ever had a case of the piles?"

Again he did not wait for a reply. "Well, I bet lotta people who come in here's got 'em, so you tell 'em this: They should get them a jar of Vicks and get them a good-sized gob of it on the end of their finger and put that right up in there where all that burnin' and itchin' is a going on. Do that three, four times a day, and there'll be relief for 'em for sure, I kin tell ya that much, missus. It's what I'm gonna do soon as I leave here." He smiled.

The clerk stood in stunned silence, her mouth agape, staring at the bib-overalled, toothless man whose voice sounded like he'd been gargling with lye water all of his life, who had just spewed forth such unusual, explicit instructions on how to deal with what would generally be considered a mostly private malady.

She struggled to regain her composure. "Wha . . . Wha . . . Well, sir, I'll certainly keep that in mind. Thank you very much."

"Don't mention it, missus." Whimpy pocketed his change. "Only glad to help out where I kin."

In the coming years, "the drug store lady conversation" was mentioned to Whimpy several times. His answer was always the same: "Hey, boys, it's a fact of life. I was just tryin' to help her out. What's wrong with that?" He'd chuckle some and shake his head.

Uncle Whimpy died at the Fountain City Rest Home when he was about eighty years old. Right up until the end, he retained his sense of humor, his love for the natural world, and a healthy zest for life.

He left me all of his worldly possessions. A couple of well-worn fly rods and reels. Several jackknives. A few tattered pictures from days gone by. A pocket watch with a small leather strap attached. His mother's wire-rimmed glasses in a small case. A little rusty metal box filled with an assortment of fishing tackle. Some bib overalls and his trusty cigarette-lighting gadget.

He had not one penny to his name. No insurance policies. No retirement plan. No real estate property, no automobile, and no bills.

Most folks would have thought him to be a very poor man indeed. However, some riches cannot be measured in dollars and cents. Whimpy was never saddled with the responsibilities, cares, and worries that accompany having a wife and family, property, or the day-to-day stress of steady, gainful employment.

He saw the sun rise and set over wild places and wild things more times than most folks will ever dream of.

He left me a treasure chest filled with bits and pieces of knowledge, countless experiences of the natural world, and fond memories of a colorful old-timer, which I am able to draw from whenever I feel the need.

Uncle Whimpy gave me a priceless gift.

He was a very rich man.

Joey and her pups, 1986.
Courtesy of the author

PART II

OLD DOGS

I have never "owned" a dog. Some have been given to me by folks who no longer desire the dog's friendship or are unable to have the dog in their life for various reasons. Other dogs have come to me of their own accord, begging for a home. And yes, I have paid cold, hard cash for a couple of dogs; however, that still does not mean that I "owned" them. I simply purchased the privilege to share the rest of our natural lives together.

How could I ever "own" a friend? Someone who is always satisfied with the food, shelter, and attention he receives?

In return for these basic needs, the noble dog cares not how I look or smell, whether I'm rich or poor, handsome or ugly, old or young. My education or status in life means nothing to him. The color of my skin and the language I speak is meaningless. My dog is always happy to see me. After an hour, a day, a week, a year, the reaction is the same: jumping, barking, wagging his tail. In body language, he's saying, "Dad, I'm so glad that we're together again. Don't be gone so long again, I hope."

A dog is always ready to kiss away any cares, worries, or fears I might have. Not sometimes. Always.

I can count on my dog for loyalty, comfort, joy, friendship, and unconditional love. If one of my dogs had a bad habit, the blame could usually be traced to me. I don't believe there's any such thing as a "bad" dog.

From day one until now, sixty-five years later, I have never been without a dog. Therefore, I've never been without a best friend. I was born about four miles east of the Mississippi River, as the crow flies. There was always at least one dog, and most times two dogs, roaming about our little hill country farm. All of these dogs were mixed breeds of various shapes and sizes and colors. As is the case with all things in the great Circle of Life, each one had a special ability or talent. Each had his own distinct personality as well.

There was Brownie, a short-haired little cow dog. Wilkie was a part-Airedale cow dog. Rover had English shepherd blood and was, without a doubt, the best herding dog on our place. Teddy had the misfortune of biting into a car tire as it was turning, which bent one of his canine teeth and made it stick out of his mouth at a sharp angle. With this strange "tool," he could grab a large wayward pig by the ear and hold it in its tracks till we got there to put the pig back inside its pen. There was Spotty, a hound mix who turned up in our hay barn one fall, suffering from a gunshot wound to his hind leg. We nursed him to health and he became as fine a pheasant dog as ever took to the field. Finally, we had a rat terrier/Spitz mix named Pepper, who caught mice and rats as well as any cat. He was also an excellent squirrel hunter.

After I left my parents' hill country farm, I became a river rat. Dog friends became an even bigger and more important part of my life. I was now spending a great deal of time alone, so my swamp dogs were not only my best friends, they were my daily work mates as well.

First, there was Spook, a Lab/golden retriever who was given to me. For a short while I had Spike, a springer spaniel/Lab cross who came to Big Lake Shack as a stray on a cold winter day. Next, I hooked up with Joey, a purebred black Lab whose registered name was Blue Water Billy Jo. What a magnificent water dog she was. Then I purchased another purebred Lab, officially named Black Widow. I called her Spider. At this same time, my wife's golden retriever, Traveling Travis McTavish, known as Travis, shared his life with us until his untimely death at the age of five and a half years.

These days, Webster is our dog friend. My wife, Mary Kay, rescued him from a roadside ditch twelve years ago. He is a German shorthair crossed with some sort of hound. However, he thinks he's a Lab. Webster takes to the water after a duck no matter how cold it might be, knowing full well when he returns to the bank, he will pay the price for having such a shorthaired coat by shivering so hard his teeth chatter like a minijackhammer, yet he is always ready to go again. He's such a joy.

With the exception of Webster, all of the dogs I've mentioned have passed on. They have completed their walk in the Circle of Life. Their days in the sun have drawn to memories and shadows.

Through all these years and all the dogs I've known and loved, not one of them has passed on by way of an "easy" death as far as the dog is concerned and certainly not for me. Those who died naturally showed how tough and tenacious they were. They fought for the breath of life with every ounce of strength they could muster. I suppose for those who died unnaturally—at the veterinarian's hospital—it may have involved less physical suffering. That process is, however, a most horrible thing for me. I recall each such experience as one of the most awful days of my life.

No matter how my dogs have passed on, each time a part of me has gone with them. That's how it feels. I can't change that. However, when I consider the incredible amount of joy, comfort, friendship, and love that each one gives in his lifetime, the good far outweighs the bad in all cases. If dogs have one glaring defect, it is that they do not live long enough.

In the following pages, I share with you the lives and times and memories of some of my dog friends. It is my most sincere hope that you enjoy traveling back through those days as much as I did living them.

3. JOEY GIRL

My friend Dick Fleming was on the phone. "Kenny, I hear that you lost old Spook a short while back."

"Yup, I did, Dick. We lived together for the better part of sixteen years, you know. One day he just kind of laid out on the grass and died."

"Sorry to hear that. It's always tough to bear such a thing. However, I have a proposition for you. My brother-in-law, Armand Snieder, breeds and runs Labrador retrievers in field trials. He's got a black Lab female that is three and is fully trained and has won a few trials. She has great papers, but he feels she's too soft to become a champion, so he's raising pups from her. She's had one litter of ten pups so far. I told him about you being a river rat and that you might be needing a swamp dog soon, and Armand said he would give this dog to you if you would be willing to raise some pups from her. He'd get the pups. You'd get the mother dog. What do you think of that, Kenny?"

"Well, Dick, I thank you for thinking of me. It sounds good. However, the whole thing is an awful lot to digest on the spur of the moment. I'll need some time to think about it and talk it over with my wife. I'll get back to you soon."

The deliberation began. The dog was three years old. Would she ever accept a new home, a new workmate, a new lifestyle complete with places and things she had never encountered before? We had no experience as far as the raising of pups was concerned. Where would they be kept, what to feed them, how to care for the mother? The mother—my God, I didn't even know her name!

A month later, on a gray, snowy February day, Dick Fleming and Armand Snieder pulled up to the front gate of our little four-room cottage in Buffalo City, Wisconsin.

I went out to greet them. Dick introduced me to Armand, who then went to the back of his Suburban truck, swung open the doors, and opened a dog cage. A beautiful, sleek, medium-sized black Lab jumped down to the street.

Armand said, "Sit," and the dog sat quietly by his right leg.

"This here's Blue Water Billy Jo," Armand said. "She'll answer to the name Joey. If I used her full name, her turn would be over in a field trial before I got it all said." He chuckled. "Come over and meet her, Kenny."

I walked over and slowly stroked her silky head. "Hi there, Joey girl. You're sure a beauty." I patted her back, and she swept the street clear of snow beneath her tail.

Armand told Joey to stay. Then he took a retrieving dummy from the truck, walked down the street a full block, laid the dummy down in the snow, and came back.

He stood alongside Joey, bent down, pointed toward the dummy, swung his arm back and forth past her head in that direction, and said sharply, "Back, Joey."

She took off like a shot out of a cannon. I'd never seen a dog run so fast in a perfectly straight line. When she was about halfway to the dummy, Armand gave one long, sharp blast from a whistle hanging around his neck on a lanyard.

Joey came to a skidding stop in a cloud of snow, turned toward Armand, and sat down, awaiting further instructions. These came in the form of a couple of long overhead forward motions of his arm toward the dummy and several short toots on his whistle.

Joey was off again running full bore. Once again, a single long blast of the whistle brought her to a "stop, look, and listen" mode. This time, Armand's hand signal went to the right. A few short whistles and Joey went to her right, and a minute or so later, she had the dummy in her mouth and was running headlong back to him. When there, she promptly sat down at his right side. He took the dummy from her, patted her head, and said, "Good girl, Joey."

Good girl, Joey—that's all! Holy moly, this dog was a machine! Talk about mind control. I'd done seen the ultimate demonstration, bar none!

Armand asked if I'd like to "handle" her a time or two.

"Thanks, but no thanks," I said. "Not right now. I've got to get back down to the swamp to check some rat traps."

All the while, my friend Dick Fleming just kind of stood off to the side with his hands deep inside the pockets of his hunting coat, wearing a slight grin upon his Santa Claus look-alike face. Yes, he did have a twinkle in his eye as well.

Armand brought Joey up our limestone steps, sat her down by the front door of our little cottage, shook my hand, and said, "A pleasure to meet you, Kenny. We'll be in touch. Dick, let's head back north to Eau Claire."

"So long, my friend," Dick said. "Don't hesitate to call Armand or me if you have any questions about Joey. Good luck. I know it will work out."

I followed the two of them down the steps. "Wait a minute—I never said I'd take this dog. Hold on here. You can't just leave this poor dog sitting here with strangers and walk away from her like this. What in Sam Hill is going on?"

"It'll work out just fine," Dick said.

They got into their truck and drove away as if they had just left some sort of cardboard box at my doorstep instead of a living, feeling creature.

I turned toward the gate. There sat Joey exactly where Armand had "placed" her, quietly waiting like a mouse in a cupboard when the door is suddenly opened.

I walked up to her. "Well, girl, I hope everything and everybody will suit you around here, 'cause it looks like we might be together from now on. Come on, Joey."

She didn't move.

I thought back as to how Armand had used one-word commands. "Come," I said, slapping my hand on my leg and walking away. She followed me this time, and I began a tour around our six-lot yard, with Joey sniffing, peeing, and scratching as her mood and necessities dictated.

My wife at the time, Faye, came outside to join us in our inspection of the property. Joey readily took to Faye as a friend.

Afterward, we opened the front door and tried to coax Joey into our cottage. It was apparent that she had not been indoors very often before. She came inside but crouched with her fur standing on end as she sniffed every nook and cranny.

Faye and I talked over the situation.

"I never dreamed those guys would leave this dog here at the drop of a hat the way they did," I said. "What are we gonna do now? Armand said to keep in touch. I have a hunch that we're gonna be 'in touch' before the night is through. Good Lord, this poor dog is gonna miss its home, ain't it now, Faye?"

Faye thought a minute. "Why don't you take Joey down to the swamp for a while and get acquainted with one another. It's such a strange place for her, so I think she won't have time to get homesick with all the sights and smells she'll encounter there. Why don't you try it, Kenny?"

An hour later, I was already in touch with Armand by phone. "Armand, how in heck do you get Joey into a vehicle?" I asked.

He chuckled. "Kenny, you simply say two words: kennel up."

I went out into the yard, by the old red barn, where my car and Joey were both "parked," opened the back door, and said, "Kennel up." Joey leapt into the back of my car as if she had lived there all of her life.

Twenty minutes later, we rolled to a slow stop in front of Big Lake Shack. Joey and I got out of the car and began a ten-year partnership of work, play, love, and friendship, despite all odds against it to the contrary.

During the remainder of that winter, we traveled the lonesome ice pack checking muskrat, mink, and beaver traps together. Our nights were spent skinning critters under the dim light of kerosene lamps next to the penetrating warmth of the wood-burning stove.

Joey never turned her nose up at the leftovers of my backwoods suppers, and she snored peacefully upon her bed of blankets and quilts on the floor alongside my "Boar's Nest" bunk at Big Lake Shack.

Come spring, Armand called to find out if he and his wife, Margaret, could join Faye and me for a day of morel-picking in the nearby hills.

"By all means," I said.

The following Saturday, we set forth with walking sticks, day packs, lunch, water jugs, and high hopes for our 'shrooming expedition. It was the end of the first week of May. Our little mushroom gang spread out over a wooded hillside, about thirty yards apart, checking out the dead elm trees. We walked for an hour without finding anything, Joey by my side at the bottom of the hill. The woods were alive with a beautiful chorus of birdsongs. Each one sang in its own key, each with a different set of notes, yet they all sang at the same time. It was so lovely and soothing. It sounded just right, perfect—a natural thing. I couldn't help thinking how horrible it would sound if people followed the birds' example. Why, you wouldn't be able to stand it! With everybody singing their own song, each in a different key and all singing at the same time, it would be enough to send the listener over the edge for sure. I wondered what the difference was.

My wandering mind snapped back to the task at hand when Armand called, "Hey, guys, I found a bunch up here." He did not have to sound the alarm a second time. There was a sudden scrambling of footsteps up the steep hill.

Armand was at the top waiting. Joey made it up the hill past everyone to join her old friend first. She wagged her tail and licked his hand. He scratched her ears and patted her side in greeting.

When we all finally got to Armand, we found he had not been waiting: He had been picking, big time! Already there were at least thirty nice, fat, yellow morels in his bag. Not to worry, though. There were mushrooms scattered in a fifty-foot circle under a huge old American elm whose bark was just beginning to crack off from the ravages of Dutch elm disease. After a certain amount of confusion and chatter, we each settled down to the bent-over work of harvesting the morels all around us. Later, after collecting the last mushroom within our sight, we took our lunches from our packs.

Joey came over to me right away to share my sandwich. She did so in a ladylike fashion, taking each piece gently from my hand, never begging, simply waiting patiently for the next morsel to be offered. Until she came to live with us, she had never eaten anything but dry dog food in her entire three years of life. By now, however, after only a couple of months, she had acquired a healthy taste for people food as well.

Next, I fished a small plastic bowl from my pack, poured it full of water, and set it on the ground. Joey drank with gusto.

I looked over at Armand. He smiled at me and nodded.

After lunch, we followed a different hillside back to our cars. We picked a few more mushrooms; however, for the most part, we simply enjoyed the woodland bounty of spring. The plants and birds, the squirrels and chipmunks. The fresh air that filled our lungs. The warm southern breeze. The bright sunlight that caressed our faces.

Often, we stopped to sit beneath a tree. We'd close our eyes, then turn our faces up at the cloudless sky, listening to the heartbeat of the reawakening hill country. And best of all, we said little or nothing to each other and certainly not to Joey. No calling for her was necessary, as she was always close by my side. There were no commands for her to hear. There was no retrieving work for her today. With no car traffic and no chance of meeting up with other people or dogs, there was no need for a leash or collar to control her every movement.

There was no kennel waiting to confine her at Big Lake Shack or at the Buffalo City cottage. Free—she was free to sniff the air, to roam the hills, to read the daily newspaper of natural life: *Ah, a chipmunk buried a cache of seeds here and a rabbit slept under this brush last night. Hmm, a coyote peed on this stump yesterday. There have been quite a few deer down this trail recently and one of them has a sore hoof. There is the smell of a little blood 'cause of it. Wasn't so long ago a squirrel went up this tree. Wow, an owl must have caught a mouse here.*

How inept her people friends were. We had no knowledge of any of this.

Back at the car, Armand said, "Joey's got just the kind of home I'd hoped for her. Notice how she stuck close to you all day. Yeah, she was glad to see me. However, she clearly belongs to you now and I'm happy about that. I'll be in touch about getting her bred for more pups."

Armand and Margaret thanked us for the day's adventures and drove off to Eau Claire with minds at ease.

That summer was spent running set lines for catfish and pole fishing for sunfish, perch, walleye, and bass. Oh, how Joey loved to go fishing! She whiled away countless hours lying on her old blanket in the bow of the canoe in the cool river bottom shade of overhanging silver maples, river birch, and swamp white oaks. From time to time, she would leave the canoe to nose about the wooded islands and perhaps swim a lap or two across a deep, meandering slough.

When a hooked fish splashed on the surface of the water, Joey's attention was riveted. She'd look back at me as if to say, "Dad, did you throw something out there that I ought to be retrieving for you?"

At times, as soon as the fish broke water and before I could tell her to stay put, she dove in, swam swiftly to her "mark," and began to swim in ever widening circles, hoping to catch a glance or a whiff of her quarry. By now, I was reeling the fish toward shore, where it would set about splashing and thrashing in earnest. Joey would suddenly appear behind it, chasing it to and fro, back and forth into ever shallower water, where she would somehow eventually grab the fish directly behind the head, lift it from the water, wade up onto the bank, and drop it at my feet. Then she would shake off a spray of water everywhere, look proudly at me, then at the fish flopping at my feet, and back at me again. She was one happy, proud, carefree dog who loved this fishing game.

I, on the other hand, was one nervous, uncomfortable, fearful angler. I wasn't worried about losing the quarry. If we lost a fish due to her actions, so what? There were plenty more to be caught. We weren't starving to death.

It was the thought of her getting tangled in the line or embedded with a fishhook that worried me. I tried to discourage her from helping me land fish, to no avail. And eventually, I learned that as long as I kept the line tight, she could see where it was and avoid it without fail. And she invariably grabbed the fish in only one place—directly behind the head—thus avoiding the fishhook as well. After she had the fish in her mouth and lifted it free of the water, she rarely lost her grip, even though she would, at times, have to wade up- or downstream to find easier access to the bank where I stood.

It was a most unusual sight indeed: her wading along, me feeding out line until she gained the bank, then me reeling in line as she proudly walked toward me. It was as if I had caught a black Lab who just happened to have a fish in her mouth.

Joey had two definite rules about fishing that she followed without fail. First, she never, ever tried to retrieve a fish from a boat or a canoe. The second thing was a small fish like a sunfish, crick chub, or perch, which I could raise pretty much directly out of the water, wasn't worth bothering with.

Back in those days, I had a few regular clients whom I guided in the spring, summer, and early fall on trout-fishing trips. One such person was a hospital administrator from the Twin Cities by the name of Bill Botnan. Bill came down to my place one day unannounced. He always claimed that was the best way to find me, 'cause otherwise I'd run off and hide on him.

Bill asked if there would be a chance of going to northeast Iowa on a trout-fishing trip for a day or two. I told him there was a damn good chance and let's go do it. Only thing was I had me a new dog and would he mind us taking her along?

Bill met up with a bounding, wiggling, tail-wagging bundle of short black hair called Joey, who sat right down by his side and licked his hand.

"Kenny, we always took old Spook along with us," Bill said. "Why not this little black beauty? She'll be retrieving ducks for me in the fall. I might as well get to know her right now, don't you think?"

I allowed as how I thought that was all well and good. "Only thing is, Bill, this here dog is not your run-of-the-mill duck dog black Labrador retriever type. She's a fish retriever as well, and if you hook a sizeable trout, she'll retrieve it for you sure as the sun comes up in the east. Thought that might make you a little nervous, to say the least."

Bill gave me a little sideways glance and chuckled. "You old rat, you've got a thousand ways of stretching the truth and pulling a man's leg. I'll believe that one when I see it."

We loaded our gear in the trunk, put an old blanket on the back seat, put Joey up onto it, and set off down the road in Bill's long, shiny black Cadillac.

That evening, we fished the upper reaches of Village Crick near Lansing, Iowa. Although we had caught several trout a foot or so long, Joey showed no interest in them, preferring to wade and swim at her leisure in the cool, clear, rippling waters.

"I thought I heard you say that this dog was a fish retriever, Kenny." Bill grunted and smiled a little as he cast his bait into a heavy riffle that slacked off into a deep, blue-green pool.

A couple of minutes later, Bill's rod tip bent sharply down to the water and the long, wide, silvery side of a rainbow trout rolled and splashed in the blue-green pool.

In a flash, Joey was in the water, churning and chugging her way to her mark. Before she got there, the fish leaped off to the side. Now Joey headed in that direction, swimming in circles. Again the fish jumped and rolled, this time closer to the bank, where Bill was frantically taking up slack line. Joey quickly moved in behind the fish, which was now turned on its side in the shallow water. Just as she made a slashing dive for the fish, Bill hollered, "No! No! Please don't!"

It was too late. Joey lifted the twenty-inch rainbow from the water in a viselike grip directly behind its head and waded toward the bank. As luck would have it, she found an easy exit near Bill. She dropped the fish at his feet, shook herself, and sat looking at him as calm and cool as a jug of lemonade setting in a refrigerator.

Bill, however, was anything but calm and cool. He lunged and pinned the beautiful rainbow trout that was flopping in the grass at his feet.

By this time, I had made my way over to his side. His quivering hands removed the hook from the fish with a set of fishing pliers. In turn, the pliers were used to rap the fish sharply on top of the head several times in rapid succession.

The trout now lay still, its silver side colored by a crimson streak in the lush, verdant grass.

Bill cranked up his line, fastened his hook to the cork handle of his rod, carefully laid his pole to one side, and sat down on the bank. I sat down beside him. His breathing had now become slow and measured. His forearms rested upon his knees. He turned a bit to look at me. His eyes were the size of silver dollars. His mouth moved to form words; however, the only word I could understand was "Jesus."

He began again. "Sweet Jesus, that was the most unbelievable experience of my life!"

He thought further. "I spent my early twenties in North Africa getting shot at during World War Two. After that, I got an education by way of the GI Bill. I landed a job that took me all over the world, among all kinds of people. Nevertheless, Kenny, this experience along the banks of Village Crick with your pal Joey was the damnedest thing I've ever seen, bar none."

"I told you she'd retrieve a sizeable fish for you. She don't mess with anything else, my friend."

Bill laughed. "It makes both you and her hard critters to figure out. How'd you ever teach her to do that?"

"It was the other way around. She started doing her 'fish thing.' I tried to put a stop to it and couldn't. So I figured, what the heck, she enjoys doing it and it seems to work out all right if I do my part the way I should. She taught me, and hey, I don't have to drag a net around through the brush and tall grass and weeds. She's as good a fishin' pal as anybody could ever ask for. Another thing is, she won't tell on me if I stretch the size of a fish a little. That's more than I can say for most of my two-legged fishing pals." I chuckled and hugged Joey.

Over the course of the coming years, Joey would perform her "fish thing" for a great many anglers, in varied situations and places, without fail.

One such performance comes to mind, however, when things got a little hairy for everyone involved.

A man by the name of John Walter and I were fishing trout in a deep bridge hole on Winnebago Crick in southeastern Minnesota. We were fishing from the bridge itself, because the banks were steep and slippery. The water was crystal clear. We could see a large trout finning away the day in the shadow of a bridge piling. John kept drifting his bait past the resting trout, which showed no interest in his offering whatsoever until about the tenth drift, when it slowly swam over to intercept the bait. The great trout opened its mouth, flared its gills, shook its head, and the bait disappeared, all in the blink of an eye.

John reared back on his fly rod and the battle was on. At first the big fish hugged the bottom, bulldogging its way around the deep pool. This was a good thing, because although Joey knew there was a fish on, she had not had any indication as to whether her help was needed.

During the next few seconds, her indecision ended. There was an explosive splash as the fish broke water. Joey cleared the end of the bridge in three gigantic bounds and skied down the steep, slippery bank on her butt. She made a water entry that was a long way from graceful.

Several problems loomed large. The first was the fact that there were steel supports running from the top of the bridge to the railing. If John wanted to move the fish toward the bank, he needed to reach around the supports and switch his rod from one hand to the other. This he did. The second bad thing was that the pool dropped straight off the bank into deep water. There was nowhere to beach his fish or for Joey to pin it down. It was then that the third, and by far the most problematic, thing occurred. Although I didn't see it happen, somehow Joey had gotten her fish grip on the big trout. I heard about the problem first, because suddenly John's reel was whining, squealing, and screeching. John's face was set in a sweaty grimace, his teeth tightly clenched, both of his hands holding his arched fly rod in a white-knuckled grip as if he had a shark on the other end.

I looked over the side of the bridge railing and saw Joey swimming swiftly downstream with a lunker trout in her mouth.

For the first time since the whole fracas began, we spoke. "Stop her, Kenny! For God's sake, stop her!" John pleaded. "I'm running out of line. I'm well into the backing already."

"Cut the line," I answered. "She'll take the fish up onto the bank safe and sound for you."

"Cut the line? Are you nuts? I should cut the line when I've got the biggest trout on the end of it that I've ever caught in my life! No way, buster!"

Just then, Joey ended our discussion by wading up onto the thick grassy bank at the far end of the pool.

I hollered, "Stay, Joey, stay there, girl!" And she did.

John and I made our way down to where Joey was standing guard over her prize: a twenty-six-inch, seven-and-a-half-pound German brown trout. We unhooked the fish, threw the line out into the crick, and walked back to the bridge, where John wound up his line.

After putting his trout into the ice cooler, John knelt next to Joey, stroked her head, and repeated these words several times: "Good God Gerty, what a girl you are, Joey! What a day this was!"

Joey's fish thing was not only practiced on hooked fish. Sometimes I caught a fish that was too small to be placed in the fish bag to eat. There were times when I would unhook it and release it carefully back to its home, only to have it turn belly-up a few minutes later and begin to float off with the current. Joey would then be called to my side, where I would give her a line with my hand in the direction of the floating fish and say, "Fetch 'em."

Off she'd go, and in no time at all, she'd deliver the dead fish to my hand. Therefore, the fish ended up in my frying pan instead of being raccoon or mink fodder.

Now, I realize—as well as or better than most—that all creatures in the great Circle of Life need to eat. It seems to me, however, that to release a hooked and landed fish that shows no outward signs of injury, in all good intentions, and then have it turn belly-up to float away beyond retrieval is a terrible waste of a precious resource. Joey alleviated many a guilty feeling for me.

Our first autumn together was spent hunting ducks to fill our larder for the coming winter. Joey and I both had a lot of adjustments to make. Joey was used to whistle commands; I had never used a whistle and refused to do so now.

Many times in years past, I had sat quietly in marshes and swamps, enjoying the peaceful beauty of a new autumn day being born, with my dog by my side. Dusky silhouettes and whispering wings betrayed the presence of ducks overhead. I waited, however, for that one close-up, dead-in-the-air shot that would put meat in the roaster come nightfall.

Suddenly, in the distance, a volley of shots would ring out, then another volley, and then maybe a single shot or two. This was followed by shouted commands. Then dog whistles pierced the air in various pitches and series of blasts. Now tempers began to flare. Commands were delivered by way of hollering and screaming, not only at the dogs but between hunting partners as well. Certain words of foul language found my ears. It was as if some sort of battle was being fought. I guess in a way it was a battle between dog and person.

The person was saying, "Hey, you dumb dog, I paid good money for you, trained you over and over, built you a kennel to live in, fed you the best dog food money can buy. We both saw the duck I shot fall into those weeds across the pond. I'm sending you to exactly where it is. Now why in Sam Hill can't you find it for me?"

The dog, in turn, is thinking (and yes, folks, I do believe that dogs think), "Jeepers creepers, will you lay off that whistle and quit hollering at me for one minute. I'm so nervous and mixed up now that I don't know which end is up. I've been over there and the duck is not lying where you think it is. It's wounded and it's moved into hiding. I wanna go back over there again, only this trip, be quiet and give me some time to sort out where it went, and I'll bring it back to you as soon as I find it. It's so blasted thick with vegetation, I can't see my foot in front of my face back in there. I've got to go by what my nose tells me, and that's slow going when I'm in mud up to my belly. So kick back and ease up some, pal, and I'll do my very best to find that duck."

After being privy to a whole lot more of these battles than I ever wanted to be, I made up my mind that I would never, ever engage in, nor subject my dog/friend to, such confrontational mayhem.

It would naturally follow, as mentioned earlier, that Joey (who was trained in the traditional manner) and I (who would not follow some of that training) would have certain problems afield. This we did. However, there were only two problems that needed to be ironed out.

As long as the duck fell dead, things went like clockwork. It didn't matter how far away or what type of cover it fell into. She was an incredible marker. She would mark where the duck fell, I would softly say, "Fetch 'em," and the duck was brought to hand.

It was wounded ducks that presented the first problem to us. I say "us" because the trouble lay mostly with me, not Joey. If I had shot the duck down dead, Joey's problem would never have had to be reckoned with. Now, I have been shooting at feathered meat since I was big enough to swing a shotgun in the air and discharge it safely. In my case, as of today, this translates into about fifty-six years of practice.

They say that practice makes perfect. This, however, has not proven to be true for me. Over the years, I have had more than what I consider to be my share of "crooked barrel" days, when the simplest, easiest shot is missed. Often, I have been tempted at such times to open a shot shell to see if the thing had any BBs inside it.

A clean miss is not a bad thing: The bird flies away unhurt and wiser. However, crooked barrel days can involve striking the bird with the fringe of the shot pattern. This is a bad thing, for the bird now falls wounded—or, in hunting terms, crippled—very much alive and, at times, a long way from where it was shot.

Joey would mark the injured bird, and I would send her after it. If she did not find it, shortly she would come out to where she could see me, looking, true to her training, for directions from me in the form of voice commands, whistles, or hand and arm signals, none of which I brought forth. I could not offer her any advice. She was in the general area of the downed bird. Now she simply had to use her own head and sharp senses to find it. I could and would not be able to help her in any way, so I sat down on my hunting pail or against a tree and ignored her.

The first few times this happened, she came back to me without the duck. I knelt down to her eye level, stroked her head, and explained, "Joey girl, there's a duck down over there. I can't help you, so you've got to go back there and find it yourself. Take your time. I know you can do it. Fetch 'em up now, Joey girl."

And damned if she didn't do just that.

The second thing we had to figure out as partners and friends was how we could separate from each other a little now and then. When hunting, if I sat down, she sat next to me. If I walked, she was always a couple of steps behind me. As a matter of fact, several times I stopped quickly, only to have her run into the back of my legs. She was as constant as a shadow. Monstrous mountains of mulberries, I wanted a dog, not a robot!

As we walked, I began to tell her, "Go ahead, Joey. Go ahead, girl." She would then run ahead of me a short ways, and I praised her.

One day, a couple of gray squirrels were foraging in the autumn leaves ahead of us. Suddenly, she ran after them, and they scampered up a tree, where they proceeded to scold Joey. She jumped up and down at the base of the tree and barked.

Barked, my God, she actually barked! It was the first time I had heard her do so in the nine months we had been together.

That winter, Joey traveled with me each day all over the swamp to check my trap lines. In late February, Joey went into heat. Armand came and took her to a stud dog to get bred. Armand said the pups would be born in about sixty days. Pups—holy mackerel, what do we do?

Armand allowed as how "There's nothing to it, Kenny. I'll bring down all the stuff you'll need, and I'll walk you through the entire process step by step. Don't you folks worry about a thing, okay?"

The sixty days of gestation went by all too fast. Now we were in the final day, and Joey was nervous and began to build little birthing nests next to the woodpile. Armand arrived with a whelping pen, which we set up in one of the four rooms in our cottage. The pen was a four-foot-square by two-foot-high plywood contraption that had four boards fastened around the inside, just high enough off the floor so the pups could crawl under them to keep from being smothered when Joey lay down.

The whelping began around eight o'clock that evening. It was amazing how Joey licked each newborn pup dry tenderly and lovingly. Then the pup would latch onto a nipple to nurse contentedly. By midnight, nine pups had arrived. One of them had a deformed head and was dead at birth. So there were eight wriggling, squirming, grunting black Lab pups in the pen and one tired, happy mother.

Armand assured us that Joey would come and go from the pen for food and water and go outside as she needed to. He also told us that she would clean up after the pups until they began to eat solid food. And that I should take the whole litter to the veterinarian to get their shots and to have their dewclaws removed in the next ten days or so. He warned us that Joey would, in all probability, lose a great deal of her hair in the coming days, 'cause that's what had happened when she had whelped her first litter.

He asked if there were any other questions and bid us goodnight. On his way out the door, he added, "Don't hesitate to call me."

I thought to myself, "Poor Armand, you're gonna wish you never said that, my friend." He wasn't a mile down the road and I already felt as if I should call him.

I was certainly no stranger to the birthing of animals. Having been born and raised on a hill country farm, I had grown up in the midst of the life-and-death processes of every farm animal from cows, horses, and pigs to sheep, cats, and dogs.

This, however, was an entirely different situation. This involved my working partner, the very best friend I had in the whole wide world. I would never forgive myself if I failed to do the right thing and it cost Joey her life.

I needn't have worried. Right from the first, Joey was healthy and took care of her pups like the good and experienced mother she was. When she'd leave the whelping pen, the pups would whine and complain for a short while, then one by one they would pile on top of each other until they had formed a pitch-black, furry mound of snoring, grunting little bodies. Upon her return, Joey would stand outside the pen looking in for a moment or two. Suddenly, the pups would all awaken and squeal and whine and yelp. They had caught the scent of their mother. She would then enter the pen by stepping over the side. After carefully turning around several times, she would lie on her side. She had sounded the dinner bell, and the rush was on. Each pup jostled and pushed and shoved until it had found a nipple to its liking.

Several times, Faye and I noticed that the runt of the litter, a tiny female, was unable to push her way into the lunch line, so we helped her to do so. We dipped the tip of her tail in red fingernail polish and named her Sadie. Now at a glance we could tell if Sadie was getting her fair share of sustenance.

Eventually, it was time for shots and dewclaw removal. I loaded the pups into a good-sized wicker laundry basket, which I placed on the back seat of my old car, and headed south for Doc Dammen's veterinary office in Winona, Minnesota.

I was just crossing the interstate bridge from Wisconsin to Minnesota when the pups grew restless. They had been quietly sleeping in the blanket-lined basket until then. Now they began to claw and climb their way out of the basket, yipping and squealing all the way.

Doc's office was still several miles away on the west end of town. I had to maneuver my way through a number of stop-and-go lights, and I was grateful for the light amount of traffic I encountered, because my attention was definitely being distracted, to say the least.

Finally, I arrived at Doc's office and gathered up the pups—whoops, there was one missing. It had crawled under the front seat. As I carried them inside, they were still in their restless state of mind, until Doc and his assistant got a hold of them. Now each pup became as quiet as a mouse. Maybe it was the medicine smell in there or the strangers handling them. Nevertheless, even when each pup got its shot and had its little dewclaw clipped from the inside of its two front legs, there was nary a whimper.

As I headed out the door, Doc said, "My, my, what a well-behaved litter of pups you have there. Have a good day now, Kenny."

As I carried my basketful of babies to the car, a little elderly lady with a French poodle on a leash stopped beside me on the sidewalk, looked into the basket, and said, "Oh, aren't they the cutest little angels."

At the car, I debated whether to put the basket on the front or the back seat. If I put them in front and they became restless again, I didn't think I could deal with eight pups on the loose and still be able to drive safely. I figured after their vet ordeal and considering how they were now, they would make the trip home in relative peace and quiet. They went into the back.

Wrong! It was the time of day when the city of Winona experiences its version of rush-hour traffic. I was stopped at an intersection with cars all around me when the pups began to exit the basket and enter their restless mood.

Have you ever driven in heavy traffic in an old jalopy with a back seat full of pups on the loose who are lonesome for their mother and have sore butts from shots and two sore front legs? The sight is bad enough, but the sound is worse! Their tiny voices joined together in a high-pitched, eardrum-piercing chorus that sent shivers throughout my entire body. Somehow I managed to navigate through the city and across the bridge back into Wisconsin.

Several times as I drove north on Highway 35, a car would pass me. The people in the car, whom I did not know, were smiling and waving and pointing at my car. I looked in the rearview mirror and saw at least three pups cavorting by the rear window. My mind conjured up visions of pups hurtling through the air toward certain injury or even death.

I pulled the car onto the shoulder of the highway and collected the pups. I held each one to my chest and stroked it for a moment before returning it to the basket, and we were back on the road again. We hadn't gone but a few miles when the puppy chorus of yipping and whining and howling and squealing began again, in earnest. This time, they hit octaves and notes that even the finest soprano in the world could not muster! I don't know about shattering crystal. I do, however, know about shattering nerves—mine, in this case!

In no time at all, they were once again distributed throughout the back-seat area, including the rear window ledge. I thought to myself, "At least they can't get up in the front by me."

Wrong again! I heard some scratching under the front seat. Suddenly, not one but two of the little buggers were under my feet. One began "playing" with the brake pedal, while the other tried crawling up my right leg. The foot part of said leg was trying to operate the accelerator. In a jiffy, I had a deeper understanding of the term "lead foot." With one hand, I groped about and removed the leg climber, placing the pup on the seat beside me. Now I was able to take my foot off the gas pedal. I looked in the rearview mirror. No cars close behind me—good.

Next, while watching the road ahead, I used both feet to pull the floorboard rascal toward me. Then I got one foot on the brake, and—being mindful of the safety of the rear window acrobats—pulled the car to a slow halt on the side of the road.

I didn't know whether to laugh or cry. So I took a deep, ragged breath and laughed long and hard. That always seems the better of the two choices.

Then I went into the roadside ditch and adjoining bank and cut some small willow trees and tall weeds with my trusty jackknife. These I took back to the car. While I was stuffing them under the back side of the front seat, a couple of phrases came to mind: "My, what a well-behaved litter of pups you have there" and "Oh, aren't they the cutest little angels?"

I laughed again. It was not a mirthful laugh, however.

Once more we began our nightmarish trip home. I blocked out everything inside the car and focused on the odometer. The countdown began: five, four, three miles to go.

Ah, thank you, sweet Jesus, home at last! Talk about a basket case.

In five minutes' time, the pups were in the whelping pen nursing happily, while Joey licked each one carefully and gently. Life was good again.

That evening, Faye asked me how things went at the vet's office. I told her it went just fine. There was no mention of the trip there and back. I left it at that. Sometimes a half truth is better than a full one.

During the next six weeks, Joey weaned her pups. Each time one would attempt to nurse, Joey would gently take the pup's head in her mouth and simply hold it for a bit. They began to eat oatmeal soaked in cow's milk and then puppy chow. Soon they were rolling and growling and playing in the yard.

By then, we could tell them apart and we had named them all. We hugged and cuddled and played with them to no end under the ever-watchful eye of their mother.

The pups were destructive bundles of energy. They tore every plant, including Faye's flower garden, to shreds. We both agreed it would be a relief when Armand came to get them. It would be a happy day, even though we had come to love them.

Armand pulled his truck and dog trailer up by our front gate in late June. The time had come for the pups to leave.

We sat in the yard for a while and visited. Each time a pup came close to him, he would pick it up and pet it some. He was very happy about how socialized the pups were. One by one, the pups were caught and each placed in its own well-ventilated compartment inside the dog trailer. Big Boy, the largest male, was the first to go. Then Sally, a lovely female. Next Roughneck. Then Charles. From that time on, I was unable to help catch and load the pups. I sat in the grass and watched as Faye and Armand did the work. There was a lump in my throat and it wouldn't go up and it wouldn't go down and somehow it made my eyes water. Faye carried the last pup to the trailer and kissed its nose, and I saw a little red-tipped tail disappear into the compartment.

Armand thanked us, we said goodbye, and they were gone. We sat in the grass with Joey for a long time. It was one of those perfect June days: bright sun, cloudless skies, clear air to breathe, and a verdancy in the landscape. There was, however, no sense of relief and it was not a happy day for me after all!

In the coming years, Joey became a legend in her own time. Her feats as a hunting retriever were and still are talked of far and wide. Of course, stories of her fish thing have been told and retold wherever outdoors people gather along the Big River.

In her later years, Joey became afflicted with breast cancer, which traveled into her lungs. In Doc Dammen's office, on a cold, dreary February day, much like the one when I first met her, she went limp in my arms and it was over. She was thirteen and a half years old.

Armand once said, "If there is such a thing as reincarnation, I'd like to come back as the old river rat's dog, 'cause then I'd be in 'dog heaven.'"

To Joey, I say: Well, you were here, old girl, for an all-too-short ten years with me. I hope that you found a little bit of "dog heaven." 'Cause by your being here you brought a whole lot of "people heaven" to me, my dear old Joey girl.

4. Travelin' Travis McTavish

"**J**umping Jehoshaphat! Is that a dog or a pony?" The animal ran gleefully around the corn crib, past the milk house, down to the garage, then up the hill to turn tight circles around the base of the old, gnarly box elder tree at the entrance to the garden. His long golden hair rippled across his huge, powerful body like a flag on a pole.

I was standing in my future wife's farmyard in Jefferson County, Wisconsin, when I asked that question.

Mary Kay turned to me and said, "It's a dog, silly man. His registered name is Traveling Travis McTavish—I call him Travis—and he's a golden retriever. He's my little boy, you know."

Little boy? This dog was a monster! He had to weigh over a hundred pounds, and there wasn't an ounce of fat on him. His ears probably weighed two pounds apiece!

When Travis finally ran off some pent-up energy, he came over to us. I held out my hand for him to sniff, but he was wary and avoided my friendship offering.

Oh, how he loved Mary Kay. She knelt down, and Travis nuzzled headfirst into her open arms, his big feather-duster tail whipping from side to side. She whispered sweet nothings into his ear, and he smiled happily over her shoulder, big tongue hanging out the side of his mouth trying to get at her cheek.

It was the tag end of summer when I first met Travis. Maybe a week or so later, we loaded Travis and my black Lab, Spider, into the topper-covered back of Mary Kay's pickup truck for a trip to Rome Pond, a short distance from her farmstead. The day was warm, so we thought the dogs would enjoy chasing a few dummies—the retrieving kind—and a good swim.

At Rome Pond, the tailgate of the pickup dropped and a black and a golden streak of fur hit the ground running. There wasn't an idle paw to be seen for the next twenty minutes. The two dogs made their selected rounds to stumps, tall clumps of grass, and other points of interest, where they would sniff, pee, and scratch—generally in that order. First one, then the other, over and over again.

Mary Kay and I both wondered, *Where do they store all that pee?* Then we noticed they were just going through the motions. It was time to call the meeting to order.

We brought out the orange retrieving dummies. Spider knew all about this game—she was a field trial dropout. She jumped up and down in anticipation. I took hold of the foot-long cord on a dummy, wound up, and gave it a heave as far as I could out into Rome Pond. It landed with a splash, and Spider took a running jump off the bank into the pond, laid her body flat out, and began churning water toward the floating dummy.

Meanwhile, Travis had started for the water when he saw the dummy splash; however, he must have caught the black blur of Spider going past him out of the corner of his eye and decided it was too late for him. He now faced

Mary Kay as she gave another dummy a short toss into Rome Pond.

Travis watched the dummy fall, marked where it landed, lumbered off the bank, and made good progress toward it until his feet no longer touched the bottom of Rome Pond. Now he began to flounder. His front feet cleared the surface of the water and re-entered with the rhythmic sound of *plutch-plutch, plutch-plutch*. His nose was pointed skyward, and his body was entirely submerged. Talk about dog paddle—this was a classic example. His style reminded me of my own prowess in the water! Nevertheless, Travis eventually reached the dummy, took it firmly in his mouth, turned, and *plutch*ed his way to the bank. He cleared the water in one mighty lunge, dropped the dummy on the bank, shook himself off, and stood there looking at me, Mary Kay, and Spider. There was a sense of pride and happiness in his posture. His face begged the question, "Did I do good, Mom?"

Mary Kay assured Travis that he certainly had done good, over and over again. She told Spider that she had been a very good girl as well.

For the next hour or so, it was pretty much a nonstop melee of flying dummies, splashing dogs, and shouting praises—until all four of us, at about the same time, decided we were waterlogged and tired enough to call a halt to this ragtag game of ours.

We retired to a grassy bank under a nearby shade tree. Mary Kay and I laughed with sheer joy like children. Travis and Spider sprawled in the lush grass and panted steadily.

Mary Kay commented, "You know, Kenny, we're almost as wet as the dogs are. It seems as though they always wait to shake the water from their hair till they're right next to a person."

"Yup," I agreed. "It's the darnedest thing, ain't it? Guess it's 'cause they don't wanna appear selfish—hog all that nice cool water for themselves, don't you think?"

She shook her head in disbelief and smiled.

I went to the truck and returned with a small ice cooler full of sandwiches and cold drinks. Oh, how we feasted, two sandwiches apiece, and there wasn't a growl uttered by any one of the four of us.

We were resting after our meal when Spider sat up and cocked her ears forward and stared at the nearby water. I followed her gaze to see three mallard ducks, two drakes and a hen, drifting along. Spider shivered and turned to look at me. "No, you don't, little girl; it ain't hunting time yet," I chuckled.

Travis, meanwhile, also was now sitting up to look at the ducks. However, he showed only a passing interest, no more so than if the ducks had been robins hopping about a lawn.

After a while, the ducks swam off. Mary Kay and I sat with our backs against the old shade tree and listened to the wind play among the leaves.

The two dogs stretched out nose to nose in the verdant grass and took turns snoring contentedly. A few puffy clouds chased the setting sun into the far-off treetops on the western horizon. Several fish broke the surface of the water. From a distant shore, a robin heralded the coming of dusk. It had been a wonderful afternoon at Rome Pond. No one wanted to move, to break the spell; however, we had to go somewhere that night. We loaded the dogs in the truck, cranked her up, and headed for home.

There was thoughtful silence in the cab for some time. I was trying to think of a way to discuss Travis' swimming "problem" with Mary Kay. If there's one sure way to offend a person, it's to criticize her dog. Especially when she's your sweetheart, and she calls her dog her "little boy." I was between the proverbial rock and hard place, to say the least!

"Honey, it sure was a great afternoon spent with our two pals, wasn't it?"

She smiled. "Oh, it sure was! But did you notice how Travis swims? I hope he gets a better handle on that."

"In time, I'm sure he will," I answered.

Whew! She'd brought it up herself. Now I knew how a fish felt when it was taken off the hook and put back into the water!

In early October, Mary Kay and Travis came to the Whitman Swamp to join Spider and me for a duck hunt. This would be Travis and Mary Kay's first hunt together.

We met up at Big Lake Shack in the late afternoon, donned our hunting gear, and followed a two-wheeled dirt road to the south end of Big Lake. Here, Mary Kay and Travis settled into a makeshift cattail blind. Spider and I back-tracked up the lake to an old beaver dam, which was a favorite place for ducks to while away the last hours of daylight.

I began a crouched-over stalk through the high marsh grass, and Spider slow-stepped behind me. At the edge of the beaver dam, I stopped to look over the grass. Thirty yards in front of me, a small flock of wood ducks and a few teal dabbled in the water. I rose from the grass, the ducks lifted off the water, I swung the gun and shot, and a drake wood duck tumbled. Spider lunged past me to plunge into the water. Before she got to the duck, I heard two gunshots from Mary Kay's direction.

After Spider brought the duck to me, we headed toward our hunting companions.

We got there in time to see Mary Kay stroking the head of a half-golden, half-black retriever. The top half of Travis was his normal golden color; the bottom half was plastered with black, boot-suckin' Mississippi mud. His mighty tail *schlip-schlopp*ed back and forth among the cattails.

"How'd it go?" I asked.

She held up a blue-winged teal. "I got one, and Travis retrieved it for me." She turned back to Travis and said, "Didn't you, little boy?"

"That's great. Good job by all. Let's sit a spell."

We sat on a downed tree trunk near the water with the two dead ducks between us. The dogs took turns smelling each other and sniffing the ducks.

Mary Kay and I smoothed the ducks' feathers, admired their beauty, and thanked them for giving up their lives. We talked of how it was with hunting: happy and sad, good and bad, sweet and sour. This was the way of all things in the great natural Circle of Life. Gain and loss.

We took the dogs to a nearby spring hole to wash them off and joked about Spider being just as muddy as Travis—only you couldn't see it as well.

Then we walked leisurely back to Big Lake Shack, autumn leaves crunching underfoot like cornflakes. To the rear of the shack, a fire was kindled in the middle of a circle of blackened stones.

We cleaned the ducks and put them in salt water to soak overnight. A supper was prepared and eaten with all the gusto a day spent in the fresh air will bring.

Later, we sat in front of the fire on an old wooden bench. Travis lay between Mary Kay's feet and the warmth of the fire, resting his head upon crossed front feet and snoring softly. Spider lay on her side next to me. Far off in the swamp, a pair of barred owls talked over their nighttime plans from a hunting tree. Now and then, a fire spark would leap toward the stars only to disappear before it got there.

We leaned our heads back to watch our thoughts and dreams, our cares and memories, drift away with the campfire smoke on the homeless nighttime breezes.

Every so often during the rest of that fall, Mary Kay would need to travel due to her work, so Travis would stay with Spider and me in the swamp. By now we had become friends. He stuck by me like glue to one's fingers. He and Spider were more than just friends. Where one was, the other was sure to be. They were like brother and sister.

One day I shot two green-winged teal. They both fell directly in front of where Travis sat on the edge of a pond.

Before Spider could get in on the act, Travis had waded out to the ducks. Carefully, he picked up the first one, then waded out another ten yards to get the second one in his mouth as well. He turned, sloshed his way to the bank, and crawled out of the water, holding both ducks firmly. He walked over to Spider, dropped the ducks at her feet, and looked her square in the eye as if to say, "That's how it's done, little sister. Ain't no use makin' two trips for such little ducks."

He then shook the water from his coat, rolled in the dry marsh grass, brought himself up to his full height, and pranced proudly about on the bank.

In late fall, Mary Kay and I were mighty pleased to each get a nice deer during hunting season. We rely heavily upon wild game, fish, plants, and such to fill our yearly larder.

The deer were skinned and quartered and the tenderloins were removed from the rib cages at Big Lake Shack. However, we decided to do the rest of the butchering job at our little cottage in Buffalo City, a few miles to the north. The dogs were put into the back of the pickup. The venison was then piled carefully on clean plastic and covered with a large cloth for the short drive to the cottage.

When we got there, we went to the back of the truck and dropped the tailgate. There stood Travis with that hand-in-the-cookie-jar look. A foot-long chunk of venison tenderloin dangled from the corner of his mouth. He promptly dropped the meat, went to the front of the truck, and sat down innocently beside Spider.

Laughing, Mary Kay said, "What a look on his face, like 'duh, whoops, bad timing, I guess, huh?'"

"Yeah. I was stunned for a second there. He looked like he was smoking a gigantic cigar," I laughed.

We both chimed in. "Travis, Travis, what are we ever going to do with you? You big lug."

During the following spring and summer, our little family of four enjoyed a great many walks together. Often we would go to the nearby hill country valleys to follow the cricks. The dogs would find a deep, cool hole where Spider would swim gracefully while Travis *plutch*ed his way across the water. We would all sit down to listen to the murmur and gurgle of the happy waters. The sweet scent of plum blossoms wafted in the breeze. Birdsong filled the air with music.

Then we would saunter through the crickside meadows, where the dogs would chase leopard frogs in utter confusion. We admired the beauty of patches of skunk cabbage and marsh marigolds.

In these meadows by the crick, the dogs developed their favorite game of "catch me if you can." Spider would jump up and down, give a sharp bark, and take off running as fast as she could with Travis right on her tail. Across the meadow they'd go, through the grasses and wildflowers that danced in the wind— Spider's sleek ebony body taking short and fast strides, occasionally glancing over her shoulder, eyes flashing to see where Travis was. Travis galloped along behind her in great powerful leaps and bounds, ears flopping, his luxurious coat shining in the summer sun like golden kernels of wheat flowing in the breeze. Travis, however, never gained or lost any ground. He seemed to pace himself around sharp corners, zig-zags, and straightaways, always about the same distance behind his quarry—until Spider suddenly stopped.

At once, the dogs were all over each other, wrestling, growling, rolling, and playing in the lush meadow grass.

During the course of the game, the human spectators laughed and cheered: "Go, Spider, go! He's gonna catch you!" and "Faster, Travis. She's getting away from you."

The carefree, leisurely days of summer gave way to autumn. Mary Kay and Travis went home to the farm in Jefferson County.

Spider and I had much river rat work to do in the swamp. We patched canoes, cut firewood, blazed trails, and made trap stakes. Busy as we were, however, we both sorely missed the other half of the family.

Finally, a letter arrived from Mary Kay telling me she thought something was wrong with Travis. He wasn't eating like he should and seemed to have low energy. She was going to take him to the vet. Would I call her?

The next day, I made my way to a phone to make the call. Although it was good to hear her voice, the news was not good. The vet thought Travis had some sort of stomach disorder and had prescribed liquid medicine, plus pills, to be administered several times daily. Mary Kay had to be at work every day in Madison, so she was unable to administer the drugs to Travis.

That afternoon, Spider and I headed south for Jefferson County. In the evening, Mary Kay gave me instructions about the medicines and demonstrated the correct way to give them to Travis.

"At eight in the morning, you put one pill in a small ball of hamburger, lay it in the palm of your hand, and present it to Travis like this," she said. Travis swallowed the hamburger ball whole and stood there licking his lips.

She continued. "Next, you take this plastic syringe with a short rubber nozzle on the end, and you suck exactly three ounces of this yellow liquid out of this bottle. Like that." Travis sat quietly in front of Mary Kay. She reached down, and he opened his mouth slightly as she inserted the little rubber tip and pushed the plunger, all in one motion. She then held his mouth shut for a moment to be sure he swallowed the stuff.

"Good little boy, Travis," she said.

"See?" She turned to me. "There's nothing to it. It's a piece of cake."

I agreed. "Yup, I don't think I'll have any trouble gettin' the job done for you, honey."

Early the next morning, Mary Kay left for work. At eight o' clock, I took Travis into the kitchen. He sat on the floor in the same spot by the counter as he had the night before. I got a small ball of burger from the fridge, slipped one of his pills into it, stood in front of him, and whispered, "Daddy's gonna be your 'doctor' today."

I placed the burger ball in the palm of my hand, held it out to him, and he promptly gulped it down as his big tail swept back and forth on the floor. Then I removed the cover from the jar, took the syringe, and sucked out three ounces of the yellow, gooey medicine. I reached down toward Travis' head. This is when things took a sharp turn for the worse.

Instead of opening his mouth slightly, he clenched his teeth as tight as he could. I wrapped my left arm around his head in an effort to insert the tip of the syringe into his mouth. We began to struggle across the floor. I finally saw the rubber tip disappear between his clenched teeth, so I pushed the plunger.

However, before I could hold his mouth shut, he threw all 110 pounds of his weight into one mighty, open-mouthed shake of his head. It was as if a high-pressure hose had sprung a leak. A yellow spray shot out from both sides of his mouth. Then he did it again, to a lesser degree, and ran off into the living room where I could hear him rolling and rubbing his head on the carpet.

I cannot remember exactly the couple of short phrases I uttered. I am, however, quite sure that "Good little boy, Travis" was not one of them.

I stood in the middle of the kitchen, syringe in hand, taking stock of the situation. One burning question kept crossing my mind. How in the world could one dog, with two shakes of his head, spew exactly three ounces of liquid far enough, fast enough, and hard enough to place a yellow speck, daub, or splatter over every square foot of three walls, the ceiling, and the floor of a medium-sized kitchen? It was a feat of gigantic proportions!

After I entered the living room, I realized Travis' feat was even greater than I had thought. There were enough yellow stains smeared into the carpet to suggest he had completed the kitchen job with less than exactly three ounces of yellow, sticky goo. Even with that considered, I still did not feel like telling him he was a good little boy.

During the course of the day, a great many cleaning tools were brought into play: mops, scrapers, a putty knife, fine sandpaper, a stepstool, a stepladder, and an assortment of spray bottles, cans, and compounds. By evening, I had filled several water buckets with tattered sponges, soiled paper towels, and dirty rags.

As I went about my housecleaning, a couple of other phrases ran through my mind a time or two, like: "There's nothing to it," "It's a piece of cake," and "Yup, I don't think I'll have any trouble gettin' the job done for you, honey."

A glance at the clock. A quick check of the kitchen. Everything seemed okay. Mere minutes later, Mary Kay came up the steps to the front porch where Spider, Travis, and I were waiting. After hugs and kisses all around, Mary Kay asked, "Well, how did the medicine dispensing go?"

"Oh, I got the job done all right," I fibbed.

Mary Kay reached down to rub Travis behind his ears and murmured, "Was Daddy a good doctor, little boy?"

I cleared my throat. "Let's go rustle up some supper."

As we walked through the kitchen door, she said, "My, but it smells so fresh and clean in here. You cleaned up the house. Thank you, honey."

"You're welcome. I just felt I should tidy up a bit." I began setting the table.

It seemed quiet in the kitchen. I looked up to see Mary Kay rubbing something off the stove.

"What are all these yellow specks?" She put her fingers to her nose. "Why, it smells like Travis' medicine. What on Earth went on here today?" She stared at me. I knew I had that deer-in-the-headlights look on my face—rats of the river kind, foiled again!

There was only one thing to do at the time: throw myself at her mercy. I began to blame my little mishap on the fact that I possessed all the manual dexterity of a cub bear wearing boxing gloves. Then I babbled on about how bad it really was and how much better the kitchen looked now.

She held up her hands, smiled, and kissed me on the cheek. "Oh, you big monkey. You're like an overgrown kid. Now come on and tell me how it all happened." We sat down on the couch with the two dogs, and I proceeded to fill her in on the entire "event."

That evening laughter rang through the high-ceilinged rooms of the old farmhouse.

As the days of autumn drifted by, I mastered the task of doctoring Travis. However, the medication seemed to be doing little good. The big guy had little or no appetite. At times on our walks in the tree-studded pasture south of the barn, Spider would try to strike up a game of "catch me if you can." Travis would begin the chase, only to turn back and walk quietly behind us.

Once in a while, we would pat him on his side and he would wince with pain.

One evening, we decided to take Travis to another vet. We could stand it no longer. Something had to be done.

The next morning, we loaded the dogs in the truck and went north to Winona, Minnesota. Dr. Dennis Dammen had his office there. He had treated my swamp dogs for over thirty years, and I had full confidence in him.

We led Travis into the waiting room a little past noon. Doc was about to leave for lunch. We shook hands, and I introduced him to Mary Kay and Travis. Then we explained about Travis' medical troubles. Doc said, "Let's have a look at this big fella. He sure is a beautiful dog."

Mary Kay held Travis by the collar while Doc slowly ran his hands over Travis' sides. Then Doc straddled Travis' back and firmly raised up his belly and poked and kneaded every square inch of his underside. He rubbed Travis' back and petted him.

Doc finally straightened up to look at us. "I'll tell you straight out I don't like what I felt. There's a tumor, a mass, in there, and it's pretty big. Two things can be done. We can leave the thing as is; however, that will mean more agony and certain death. Or we can operate as soon as possible. Maybe I can remove the tumor and he will recover."

We told Doc we would talk it over and let him know soon. We took Travis out to the truck. He needed our help to climb into the back and whined when he did.

Mary Kay looked at me. "I just can't stand to see him suffer like this. I think we should try the operation."

I nodded in agreement, and we went back inside to make the appointment for the following morning. On the way home to our cottage at Buffalo City, we decided to walk into the Big Lake Shack.

The late October sun felt warm as it dappled the two-wheel dirt road. The sky was a deep azure framed by the colored leaves of autumn. As the road wound its way through the high ground woods along the swamp, the dogs often stopped to "read" the signs left by the passing parade of critters who lived there. However, there was no spring to Travis' step, nor to ours or Spider's. She seemed to sense that all was not right with our little family.

The sun was preparing for bed when we reached the old beaver dam on the south end of Big Lake. We sat in the dry marsh grass on the bank. Only the raucous cry of a great blue heron and the whisper of duck wings broke the silence. A few wood ducks came in low and landed with a swish in front of us. Spider sat erect, ears perked, nose twitching. Travis lay between Mary Kay and me on his belly, head resting on his front paws, eyes closed. We each put a hand on his back and stroked him softly. Time waits for no one.

In the gathering darkness, we made our way back to the truck.

At nine the next morning, we were in Doc Dammen's office. We stayed with Travis while Doc and his nurse prepared him for surgery. We petted him and scratched his ears until he was put under anesthesia.

In the waiting room, we did the usual. Drank coffee, read magazines, and fidgeted about. I've always thought one could call such places "weighting rooms." It feels as if great weights are heaped upon one's shoulders and chest.

Finally, Doc appeared. His face was solemn. He took a seat next to us and slowly began. "It does not look good. In over thirty years of practice, I have never seen a tumor of this size. It's massive. It is entwined in his intestines and is attached to some organs. I could try to remove it, but I don't think he will survive."

After a long silence, Mary Kay and I said, "We can't make him suffer any more."

We thanked Doc for his efforts and left the office carrying Travis' collar and leash. The tailgate of the truck was opened so Spider could come out on it, and there the three of us sat in a tearful huddle for a long time. At last we told Spider that Travis wasn't going home with us, patted her on the head, closed the tailgate, and started for home. We drove in silence for some time until, with tearstained cheeks, we were finally able to speak.

"He was only five and a half years old," Mary Kay said. "Travis was the most beautiful dog I have ever known. He had a kind, innocent, unflappable spirit. He had a heart of gold."

"I guess that's why they're called golden retrievers," I answered.

She nodded her head, and we drove on.

Mary and Adolf Reglin, 1902

PART III

HILL FOLK

"These people surely don't try to farm land such as this." So say those who visit here from flat lands like Iowa, Illinois, and Nebraska. Those poor folks stand in awe as their gaze travels up and down the high, steep hills.

"My word, some of those hillside fields aren't hardly big enough to be called a decent-sized garden where we come from. Why, this country would tax the energy of a mountain goat, let alone trying to make a living on it. Don't you think, Martha?"

They walk toward their car, only to be stopped by the scream of a red-tailed hawk. As they look back toward the distant hilltops, they see not only a pair of red-tailed hawks drifting in ever-widening circles but a bald eagle soaring on the homeless winds. In one of the garden-sized fields, a white-tailed doe and her two spotted fawns graze contentedly on fresh alfalfa. The scent of lovely wildflowers fills the air. A pileated woodpecker describes its territorial boundaries by rapping on a dead hardwood limb in the nearby woods. A spring-fed crick dances and gurgles its way through the narrow valley between the hills.

"Sure is beautiful here though," says Martha.

Her husband agrees. "Yes, it is. However, beauty doesn't put food on the table. I just can't understand how these people survive." The two flatlanders continue on to their car.

My granny always said, "There's two kinds of food. One kind you put in your belly, like meat and taters and such. The other kind you soak up, like a robin singin' at daylight, the smell of plum blossoms, a flock of geese flyin' and talkin' in the fall, or a whippoorwill callin' when it's gettin' dark. That kind of food you put in your heart. You got to have plenty of both kinds of food in order to live happy."

Hill folk have always survived by having plenty of both kinds of food.

Back in the 1940s and '50s, when I was growing up in the hills of Buffalo County, Wisconsin, I never knew anyone who was short of food of either kind. There were very few people who were on relief, which was doled out by the township board of directors. It generally wasn't a permanent source of food those folks needed. It was a little money to help them pay bills for a while after they had suffered a misfortune of some sort. Hill folk helped each other out as much as they could then, and they still do today.

In those days, horsepower was a common way to work the land. And I don't mean the noisy, belching, gas-guzzling monsters found under the hood of a tractor. Enormous draft horses pulled heavy farm equipment that plowed and harvested the land.

There were brushy fencerows. Animal manure was spread for fertilizer. Cows spent their leisure time in lush, green pastures. Chickens and ducks and geese roamed freely about the farmyards. Hogs still had mudholes to wallow in, and sheep and goats clipped the grass around the buildings.

Most houses had a page-wire fence around them to keep the wandering farm critters from devouring the lady of the house's flower and vegetable gardens. A small lawn was maintained with the aid of a reel-type, push-by-hand, no-motor-involved lawnmower. There was never a problem getting it started. All that was needed was a good breakfast and direct orders from Mom.

Vegetable gardens were huge, perhaps even by flatlander standards. Fresh produce was eaten all summer and into early fall. Excess garden fare was put up in glass jars and stored in the root cellar for winter use.

Farm animals and poultry were butchered when needed for fresh meat. Smoked sausages, bacon, hams, and jerky were made, plus a certain amount of canned meats in glass jars.

Most all hill folk loved to eat fish. There were trout and suckers from the cricks, carp and catfish from small rivers. A short trip took us to the Mississippi River, where the variety and number of fish were incredible. The fish were fried, baked, smoked, or pickled, as was desired at the time.

Wild mushrooms were collected in season, as well as hickory, walnuts, and butternuts. Wild strawberries, blackcaps, and blackberries were picked. Rabbits, squirrels, grouse (which we called partridge), pheasants, ducks, geese, and white-tailed deer were hunted in fall and in winter, as the local fish and game seasons dictated.

What one family didn't have and needed at the time could be bartered for from another family. Neighbors meant a great deal to one another. There was always a kindly give and take.

Most hill folk shot or trapped some furbearing critters to earn a little extra money. Some worked as hired hands on some of the big farms of three hundred to five hundred acres, which lay in the wider, more fertile valleys. Others worked as loggers or sawmill employees and cut, split, and sold firewood.

The majority did not make a lot of money. As a matter of fact, a lot of our folks lived a hand-to-mouth existence. However, my dad always said, "It ain't what you make or earn that counts. It's what you spend that'll make or break you in the end."

Quite a number of people in those times were born, cared for, and raised quite well in large families on only eighty to one hundred acres of rugged hill country land. Most of the hill folk in this area came from Germany, Switzerland, Norway, Sweden, and Poland, with a few French as well. Therefore, English was a second language for the real old-timers and their children. My parents and grandparents on both sides of the family were all born and raised as hill folk.

In this section of the book, we shall travel back in time to relive the customs, traditions, and days spent in a special place with special people called hill folk.

5. Hay Makin' and Such

"It was so hot on July 12, 1943, you coulda cracked open an egg on a steep-sided tin barn roof and not a drop of it woulda run off the eaves. It woulda fried itself on the way down." That's what Ma always said.

I don't recall the heat, 'cause that's the day I drew my first breath of life, and I never could remember that far back.

However, Ma surely should know. She was lying in her own bed among a tangled mass of birthing cloths and sheets, soaked with sweat and gritting her teeth in pain.

I would suspect one does not forget such a day, nor the conditions that existed.

Old Doc Meile had traveled five miles to our place in the hills from his office in Cochrane to deliver me.

Also there was Mary Blank, an elderly friend and former neighbor of ours who knew how to help things along.

Ma always liked to tell how "Old Doc laughed 'cause you was cryin' and carrying on the minute you was born. He took you by your feet, tipped you upside down, and slapped your behind anyway. Then he says, 'I maybe wouldn't have had to do that, but I have a feeling this spunky little fellow just might need a few more of these in the coming years. Might as well get him used to it, don't you think, Melvina?'"

Worn and sore as she was, Ma laughed right along with Old Doc and Mary Blank.

In later years, Ma said she felt the whole experience was a good sign for the start of a new life. "There was some cryin', there was some laughin', some pain, and a whole lot of happy feelings. Them are the makings of a good life."

A few hours later, Old Doc left for home.

Ma never did say how much Doc's fee was, but you can bet your life it wasn't a whole lot. The old-time country doctors were sometimes "paid" with a half-dozen dressed chickens or a few slabs of home-cured bacon and hams, maybe some fresh or put-up vegetables and home-baked bread. One thing's for sure, Doc and his wife rarely had to buy much in the way of groceries.

Old Doc left orders for Ma to pretty much stay in bed for the next two weeks to heal up proper.

The stifling heat continued. There was no air conditioning, only one small fan that moved about as much air as a traveling salesman making his pitch.

Mary Blank stayed on for the next couple of months. She did the housecleaning and the cooking for Ma, Pa, and my brother, Gerry, who was seven years old. I had my "eats" right handy at Ma's breast, so poor old Mary didn't have to bother on my account in the way of food.

She did, however, have to bother on my account in the way of cloth diapers and all the other clothes for the whole family. It was called washing clothes or just plain "wash," as in "I gotta do the wash soon." The word "laundry" was used by city folk.

Monday was wash day. In a family setting, this task fell to women and older girls. Two metal washtubs were filled with water. Usually one held hot water for scrubbing the clothes with homemade lye soap; the other held cold water to rinse the clothes. The washboard (a ridged piece of metal held in a wooden frame about two feet square) was held upright in a tub while the clothes were scrubbed up and down upon it. Then the wash was rinsed and wrung out and hung on a clothesline in the yard to dry.

In the winter or on a rainy day, the wash was hung inside the house on collapsible wooden-dowel clothes racks.

In the hill country, young men and women who were not married often worked on nearby farms for neighbors. They were called "hired men" and "hired girls" regardless of their age. They lived with the family for whom they worked and received room and board (a place to sleep and meals), plus a small wage.

During the Second World War and for a short while after, Pa had a hired man by the name of Orville Blank. His family lived on a hilltop ridge a couple miles from us. He had the kind of build that most bodybuilders can only dream of.

His powerful build was, however, the result of a whole lot of hard physical labor, coupled with genetics, rather than pumping iron on a daily basis. I called him Orbill and he called me Kanute. Some of my earliest recollections are of following Orbill around our farmyard as he did the daily chores.

One day we were in the pigpen, which had a four-foot-high oak board fence around it. While he was feeding the pigs, I went over by an old sow who must have weighed three hundred pounds if she weighed an ounce. She was lying on her side nursing about ten baby pigs. I looked at them for a minute and thought it'd be kind of nice to pet one of the little ones. So I reached down and picked one up. It started to squeal and scream like a banshee. Quickly, the big old sow was on her feet huffin' and puffin' and gruntin'. A little foam dripped from the sides of her wide-open mouth. I turned and ran toward the fence, still holding the squealing baby pig. From out of nowhere, a big, calloused hand swept the baby pig from my grasp and dropped it to the ground. Then the same hand grabbed me by the back of my shirt, lifted me straight up in the air, swung me over the fence, and set me down on the ground, all in one quick, smooth motion.

Meanwhile, Orville, who was still in the pigpen, held the metal feed pail in his other hand, as a shield between the enraged sow and his legs. The sow's teeth clicked and clacked against the metal pail. In a flash, Orville put his free hand on the top fence board and, from a standing position, hurtled the fence with all the style and grace of a trained gymnast.

He dropped to one knee, took a red bandana from his back pocket, and gave it to me.

"Now there ain't nothin' to go to work and cry about here, Kanute. There is somethin' to be learned, though. You might be too young for much of it to sink in, but I'll tell it to you anyhow."

I wiped my eyes and blew my nose.

"You see, Kanute, all little critters look nice and cute and like they'd be fun to pet and play with. But if they are with their momma, don't mess with 'em, 'cause the momma thinks you're gonna hurt 'em. All mommas are like that. They love their little ones, and they'll do anything they have to in order to keep 'em safe. Whether they're wild or tame, with critters it's all the same way."

I wrapped my little arm around his leg, looked up at him through bleary eyes, and begged, "Orbill, don't tell Ma. Don't tell her or I'll never get to go in the pigpen again."

He glanced down at me. "Don't worry, Kanute, I won't, unless you try such a stunt again. Then I'll tell her for sure."

He chuckled, and we went off to do the rest of the farmyard chores. My short little legs went as fast as they could to keep up with his long strides, so I wouldn't miss out on a single thing.

At the end of that summer, Orville Blank left our place to go back home to help his mother, father, brothers, and sister work their hilltop farm.

However, from that time on, whenever I heard a deep voice ask, "How's she goin', Kanute? Pettin' any pigs lately?" I'd answer, "Orbill, kin you still jump a board fence?" We'd laugh and visit for a while.

My parents, Willard and Melvina Salwey, bought our small hill country farm in the mid-1930s during the Great Depression. They bought it from my mother's parents, who moved down the hill from us a quarter of a mile.

Times were tough for our ma and pa even into the late '40s and '50s. So Brother Gerry and I never had a whole lot of toys of the bought kind. We didn't care about it one bit. We had the whole outdoor world around us to play in. We had animal friends galore: dogs and cats, chickens and pigs, sheep and cattle and horses.

Oh yes, the horses. How I loved the horses. By the time I really got to know them in the tag end of the 1940s, there were only three left on our farm. All three were sorrels, which means they were of a tannish brown color. Each had its own build and its own personality. All were workhorses.

Old King was nearing twenty years old. He was slow and gentle, kind and trustworthy. He seemed to sleep a lot and could be approached anytime or anyplace, taken by his halter, and led away quietly. Even so, Pa always warned us, "Never walk behind a horse or make sudden moves without them knowin' that you're there. You scare 'em and they're liable to raise up a hind foot and, quicker than the blink of your eye, they'll give you a kick that'll send you rollin' and bouncin' like a rubber ball. Even Old King!"

In his semiretirement years, King had only two jobs to perform on the farm. Every spring, as soon as the ground dried out enough, the garden needed to be plowed. Pa would harness up King, and most times, he'd let me drive him from the barn to the machine shed. I was maybe five or six years old; however, I felt real manly as I walked along behind the big old horse. I listened to his big round hooves thump the ground and to the creaking of his well-worn harness as he plodded along. And the wonderful smell of the two long, leather lines that ran from King's bridle, back through some rings on the harness, and into my hands. They were soaked through with many years' worth of human and horse sweat, plus a certain amount of harness oil.

Of course, I felt as though I needed to give some commands, seeing as I was in such a responsible position. This I did with gusto and much sternness in my voice: "Gidup, King" and "Hup there now, boy."

"You don't have to tell 'im anything," Pa said. "He knows where he's going."

When King stopped in front of the machine shed door, I just couldn't resist it. "Whoa, boy, whoa," I drawled out long and loud.

King turned his head and perked up his ears, as if to say "Whoa from what? I've already done stopped and I'm waitin', you silly little grasshopper!"

Pa hitched King to a one-bottom walking plow. Then Pa tied the ends of the long leather driving lines together and put them around his back so the lines were under his armpits. Now his hands were free to hold the two wooden handles of the plow, and he could steer the horse by applying pressure on one line or the other with his arms.

By the time Pa began to plow, I had rounded up an old pail to hold fishin' worms. Ma planted a mighty big garden, so it took quite a while to plow it. However, it didn't take near long enough to suit me. There I was, running back and forth, trying to beat the robins to the worms. And when I did nab one, I'd dream of the big fish I'd catch with it.

Kickin' clods of ground apart, smelling the pungency of spring. Warm sun on my bare head. Working with Pa and Old King. Our old cow dog Rover casting about, sniffing and peeing. Life was simple and good.

Our team of workhorses consisted of Daisy and Sally. Daisy was built more like a riding horse: tall and lean, quick and excitable, nervous and high spirited. One always had to be alert around Daisy.

Sally was pretty much the opposite: shorter and stocky, quiet and easygoing and stubborn. She was stubborn to the point where she'd simply lie down in the harness while teamed up with Daisy—not very often, but when the mood struck her, she would. The mood usually struck when the team was hitched to a wagon and waiting awhile for something to be loaded or unloaded.

Naturally, this behavior caused Pa a certain amount of frustration. However, after a little prodding and a lot of hollering, Sally would be on her feet and good to go. Pa always said, "I think that darn Sally's got a little mule blood in her for sure."

Over the years, Pa had usually worked at least five or six horses on our place at any one time. We were now down to three due to the arrival of tractors. As the old-timers liked to say, tractors were "displacing" horses—"'cause them tractors ain't really ever gonna 'replace' a horse."

The old-timer would fish a plug of tobacco and a pocketknife from his bib overalls, cut off a chunk, and work it around in his mouth while he looked far off past the tops of the hills. It seemed as if he could see the past, the present, and the future all at one time. His eyes would narrow, and his weathered face would wrinkle more than normal.

"You know, all us folks here in the hills grew up with horses. We used 'em to work the land. To carry us around on their backs from place to place. They pulled whole families of us into town in buggies and on sleighs in the winter.

"Them horses worked with us in the woods, pulling logs out of the hills so's we could saw lumber for puttin' up our barns and houses and such. They helped us get in our firewood to stay warm and for cookin'. If you was workin' with 'em by yourself, you could talk to 'em and you never felt like you was alone. We fed and watered 'em good, curried and rubbed 'em down nice, and doctored 'em up when they needed it.

"Now, there's them folks who say that tractors are better than horses. And we ought to get rid of our horses 'cause they ain't gonna be no use to us no more. I'll tell you one thing, you kin talk to a tractor till you're blue in the face and that cold, unfeeling chunk of metal ain't gonna understand a word you say. A horse will.

"Let's say you took your car or your tractor into town, and you ended up raisin' a glass or two in the saloon. On the way home, your eyes get heavy and you wanna rest some. Don't do it! 'Cause soon as you let go of them steerin' wheels, them metal monsters'll be off the road and down in the ditch. They'll never get you home by themselves. They just never kin. But a horse will.

"Another thing is the steep land in these hills. A tractor tries climbing them hills and it ain't long the tires are a spinnin'. You put the brakes on and try to go back down and you start to skid out of control. You drive along the side of the hill, and you're in danger of tippin' over. A tractor just can't do that kind of steep side-hill work. But a horse will.

"Then, too, it's about farts. A good old horse that's pullin' hard and been fed good is bound to let itself off a big old fart now and then. It's a natural thing. Might smell it for a little while if the wind's right and then it's gone. Now you take a tractor fart, that's a whole different breed of cats altogether! From the time you start the engine till you shut it off, there's just one long continuous foul-smellin' fart comin' out of that pipe. Can't be good for a person. All goes up in the air too. Can't be good no how. Smellin' a horse is like you got your nose up to a rose compared to them damned tractors.

"I don't reckon I'll ever feel about a tractor the way I feel about a horse." The old-timer would spit his chew of tobacco down in front of him, use his leather work boot to push a little dirt over it, and put his thumbs under his bib overall straps to raise them up some. As he shuffled away, he'd mutter, "Nope, don't think tractors'll ever change how I feel about horses, no, sir!"

The whispers of discontent and the breezes of change drifted throughout the hill country. There would be more to come and a challenge between the young and the old ways. New thoughts and ideas were in direct conflict with tried and proven ways of life.

Nevertheless, most hill folk clung to the old ways and only allowed the new ways to seep into their lives a little at a time. Some were good, some were bad. Each family decided which to keep for themselves. It was not a peer-pressure thing. It was a matter of the heart more than anything else.

Pa's heart was still with the horses. Yes, he did have an old tractor; however, the bulk of the work was still done by horsepower of the horse kind—living, breathing, partnership, eating, dying, friendship kind of horsepower.

Makin' hay was one of the major tasks of summertime. Daisy and Sally pulled the hay mower, which cut the hay off.

The next day, they were hitched to a hay rake, which formed windrows—long, loose ridges of hay.

After dinner, Pa checked the windrows to be sure they were dry enough to pick up and store in the barn. It was crucial for the hay to be dry. Wet hay would mold, and the farm critters would turn their noses up at moldy hay. Even worse, wet, moldy hay could catch fire through spontaneous combustion. More than one hill country barn burned to the ground 'cause folks were in a hurry to get their hay made.

When Pa gave the thumbs-up sign that the hay was ready, our Daisy and Sally went to work once again. Now they pulled a large flatbed wagon with a hay loader coupled to the back end. The hay loader was about the width of the wagon, only it was much taller and leaned at a sharp angle toward the wagon.

As we entered the field, Ma guided the horses to straddle the first windrow, one horse on each side of the ridge of hay. Pa put the loader in gear with a twist of a lever, and Ma urged the team into motion. The long tines of the loader picked up the hay, sent it up a sharp incline, and dropped it into the hay wagon. Pa and Brother Gerry each used three-tined, long-handled hayforks to pile the hay evenly upon the wagon bed. Around and around the field we went, Ma driving the horses, Pa and Gerry piling the hay higher and higher, and little old me sitting in the hay next to Ma at the front of the wagon, giving moral support to the whole crew.

The smell of the fresh hay mingled with the odor of the horses, human sweat, and the hot summertime air.

The hay loader brought aboard crickets, grasshoppers, a frog or two, and maybe a big fat toad. Fun to look at. Ma and I enjoyed their company and each other's as well. The entire family was working together. It was a good thing. However, once in a great while, a grass snake, fox snake, or bull snake was lounging under the hay windrow, sheltered from the sun, perhaps waiting for a field mouse supper. It too was "loaded" into the wagon. Most times, when Pa and Gerry saw it flop down, wriggling and writhing into the wagon, they would quickly pick it up with their forks and toss it overboard without saying a word. Nevertheless, every now and then, a snake would disappear into the load of hay.

Now, Ma was born and raised a true, dyed-in-the-wool hill country woman. From day one, she spent as much time outdoors as she did indoors. The hill country was, and still is to this very day, a snake heaven. So she was accustomed to being in their company quite often.

At some point, however, Ma developed an attitude toward snakes of all kinds, shapes, and sizes that was not friendly. As a matter of fact, she'd kill every single one she encountered. This attitude was well known to Pa and Gerry alike. Therefore, whenever a hayloaded snake escaped their frantic efforts to throw it overboard and sought refuge in the ever-growing load of hay, it behooved them to serve warning to Ma. The last thing any of us wanted was for a three-foot bull snake to suddenly emerge from the hay next to Ma and do a low crawl across the lap of her work dress—or, worse yet, to seek shelter beneath it.

So Pa would generally say, "Melvina, now there's no use to be gettin' excited, dear, but a small snake just got aboard the wagon." Pa always preferred the word small. "I'm sure it'll stay down in the bottom of the load till we get back to the barn and unload the hay."

"What?" Ma would screech, "Kenny, you crawl back to the men and get me a spare pitchfork."

"But, Ma, it's only a small one, and Pa says they're good to have around," I'd whine.

"Kenneth James Salwey, you crawl back on the load and get me a pitchfork. I don't mean tomorrow or later on today, I mean right this minute and I don't care what your pa says. He kin have all the 'small' snakes he wants crawlin' 'round him. It's what I want that counts now. And what I want is a pitchfork."

I turned tail and crawled back atop the towering load of hay, which rocked slightly from side to side with the slow rhythm of the horses' footsteps. Brother Gerry grinned through the sweat- and dust-encrusted part of his face that was not shaded by his broad-brimmed straw hat. "S'pose you're lookin' for a spare pitchfork about now, ain't you, little boy?" He offered the fork handle-first toward me and cackled like a rooster greeting the early morning sun.

Pa put one finger to his parched lips and gave a stern look to each of us. This was not the time for foolin' around.

I took the fork by its well-worn handle and dragged it to the front of the wagon. Ma was standing now, driving reins clenched in her rough, suntanned hands. "Now you watch for that snake, Kenny. If he shows hisself, you stab 'im deader than a doornail, okay?"

I nodded. In all the years I rode the hay wagon with Ma, I never had to follow through with my promise to Ma. I was glad of it and Ma felt better with me standing guard, so I guess it was a good thing on both counts.

When the wagon was loaded high enough to suit Pa, the order was given to stop. The hay loader was unhitched, and we rode atop the load of hay back to the barn.

Here, a pair of large wooden doors stood ajar at the top of a limestone and packed-clay ramp. The team of horses pulled the wagonload of hay up the ramp and into the haymow. This part of the haymow floor was made of double-thickness, home-sawn oak planks to hold the extra weight of the horses and wagon. The load was now in the center of the hay barn. An iron track ran the entire length of the haymow, just beneath the crossed rafters under the very top of the ridged roof. This was called the carrier track, upon which a wheeled device rode back and forth, attached on the inside of the barn to a one-inch rope that was tied to a large grappling device called a hayfork. The other end of the hay carrier was fastened to an even larger hay rope. This big rope ran through pulleys made of wood, then through an opening in the gable end of the barn to the farmyard below.

This was where Old King's second task in his semiretirement life came into play. I was sent to the barnyard to fetch him up for his job. I knew right where to find him. He'd be standing in the shade of a big old burr oak next to the watering tank. He'd be balancing his right hind leg up on the front edge of that hoof. His eyes would be closed, as if he were dreaming of youthful summers when he, too, was part of a team.

I'd call his name, crawl under the two-by-six oak board fence that enclosed the barnyard, and Old King would shuffle in my direction with little puffs of summertime dust kicking up from his plodding feet. I worried not that his feet, which carried over a thousand pounds of horseflesh, would be any kind of hazard. He was always kind and gentle and careful around me.

I'd reach up on my tiptoes to hug his old gray head, to pet his forehead, to feel the soft velvet touch of his lips.

Oh, how I loved my old pal King. He was everything a friend should be. Faithful, loving, trustworthy, and patient—and you could always count on his reactions to a particular situation. I took him by his halter and led him from the barnyard. King was already "dressed for work."

A full-sized horse collar fit snugly around his neck and against his foreshoulders. He wore only a light harness with one heavy leather tug on each side, which dragged behind him in the hot summer's dust. He did not need to feel the bit of the bridle today. No driving, only leading.

I brought him up to the east end of the barn, where Ma and I hooked the heavy loop of the hay rope to the harness tugs.

Pa stuck the huge hayfork into the top of the load of loose hay on the wagon. Then he hollered loud and clear, "Go ahead now." Ma and I led Old King forward. The rope grew taut as he leaned into his harness. Thirty feet later, Pa shouted, "Hold up now," and we brought King to a halt.

Inside the barn, Pa jerked the trip rope and the big forkful of hay dropped into the mow. Brother Gerry spread the hay as best he could against the walls of the barn.

It took about four or five times of stickin' the fork to unload the wagon. The rest of the load was cleaned off by hand.

Now the team pulled the wagon from the hay barn to the nearby shade of a huge, old elm tree. Old King was led into the cool grassy area as well. Pa and Gerry stretched out in the shade. There wasn't a dry spot on them. Hay chaff stuck to their sweat-soaked clothes. Haymow work was hot, dusty, muscle-testing, grueling labor any way you looked at it.

It was all in preparation for the coming of winter. Ma and I went into the house and brought back cookies and what us hill folk called Nictor. Nictor was sold and delivered to us by traveling salesmen, mostly from the Watkins Company of Winona, Minnesota. I guess the name was really Nectar, as in "the nectar of the gods." It was the forerunner of Kool-Aid, I would reckon. It came in one-gallon glass jars. And I'm here to tell you that, after adding some cold water from the hand pump, it was awful close to being the nectar of the gods on a hot, humid, midsummer afternoon during hay makin' time.

After a short rest, we all went out to the field to load another wagonful of hay and the whole process was repeated.

One day, I was leading Old King on the hay rope after Pa had hollered for us to go ahead. Where my mind wandered off to I'll never know. Perhaps I was daydreaming about a nice, fat trout in a certain fishing hole down in the crick. Maybe I was envisioning myself bringing the sights of Pa's .22-caliber rifle to bear on a fluffy gray squirrel way up in the top of a tall hickory tree. One thing I do know, however, is that I did not hear Pa holler for me to hold up.

What I did hear was a loud *kabang* when the hayfork carrier wheels hit the end of the track. Old King came to a sudden halt. There was a long silence. Then I heard hollering in the hay barn, but it wasn't coming from Pa. It was Brother Gerry who was doing the hollering. I ran for the hay barn as fast as I could. When I turned the corner, Pa was on his knees holding the top of his head with both hands. Blood ran out from under his hands and down across his face. There was a small puddle of blood in front of him on the oak-plank floor.

Gerry and I helped Pa to his feet, and he staggered out the hay barn door, then he sat down on an overturned five-gallon pail.

Gerry said to me, "When the carrier hit the end of the track, a wooden pulley broke loose and flew down on top of Pa's head."

I looked down at my feet.

Pa piped up. "Better run and tell Ma to bring the car around. Reckon I'm gonna have to pay Doc Meile a visit."

When Ma brought the car over, she wrapped a big towel around Pa's head and he lay down in the back seat.

Away they went down the gravel road with a cloud of dust billowing out behind them. Ma had the old Ford in high gear, and her foot was heavy on the gas pedal.

Gerry and I busied ourselves by cleaning up the loose hay that lay strewn upon the driveway floor in the hay barn. Then we went outside and did the same there.

While Gerry went off to feed his chickens, I pumped a pail of water. I carried it down by the granary where Old King stood quietly in the shade of the big elm tree. His eyes were closed; his breathing was slow and measured. I set the pail of water on the ground in front of him. Then I stroked his soft, moist nose.

"Were you sleepin', old pal?" I asked.

He put his mouth down into the pail and drank most of the water, then raised his head up and looked at me as water dripped off his chin.

I put both arms around his head and lay the side of my face against his. "It ain't your fault that Pa got hurt. It's mine. I was daydreamin'. You was just pullin' on the rope like you was s'posed to."

Now there was water drippin' off my chin. It was coming from my eyes. "Sure hope Pa'll be okay," I sniffled. I let go of King. He looked at me. His big, soft, hazel eyes seemed to be watery, too.

Just then Ma pulled the old Ford to a halt in the dusty farmyard. Pa stepped from the car, drew himself up as straight as he could, and adjusted his bib overalls.

Gerry and I stood alongside each other in stunned silence. Our mouths hung open, and our eyes grew wide as we stared at Pa. The middle of the top of his head was shaved clean down to bare skin, from his forehead all the way across the top and down the back as well. A thatch of long, black hair hung down on either side of what Pa, in the following days, would come to call "that blasted landing strip for flies."

Several short rows of stitches checkered the entire length of the landing strip. I guess one could have described the whole thing as a reverse Mohawk with a mini railroad track running down the center of it.

It's a well-known fact that a kid will somehow feel like laughing at the worst possible time and in a circumstance that does not call for the slightest bit of mirth or merriment. I glanced at Gerry, and a smile began to cross his face. My own lips were quivering as well. However, the sound of Ma clearing her throat long and loud, along with the hard, nasty look she gave us, stifled our strange reaction to the sight of Pa's "condition." Pa had his back to us as he gazed up at the hay rope dangling out of the gable end of the barn. He turned and said, "Boys, we got hay to make. Let's get to it."

And we did.

About a year later, on a hot summer day, Pa found us on the shady side of the old wooden silo digging for fishing worms. "Boys, the horses ain't been up here in the yard for a few days. We're gonna have to be gittin' some hay makin' done. Why don't you guys go down in the crick pasture and find 'em and bring 'em on up here to the barn." He waved his arm toward the bottom of the hill.

Why don't we go down to the crick pasture! Yahoo, Martha! That's the kind of chore we couldn't wait to get started at. We leaned our worm-digging fork against the barn. We set the pail of worms inside the cool, moist, empty silo, and we were off and running down the hill. When we got down to the crick, we followed it upstream. Oh, it felt so good to tromp along the bank, to peer down through the tall grass at the clear, sparkling, happy waters. Now and then, a leopard frog would leap from the bank to find safety in the crick. Meadowlarks and bluebirds sang from wooden posts along the fence line. Where cow and horse trails crossed the crick we found fresh deer tracks in the mud.

We sought out places where the crick ran swift and narrow. Here we took turns running as fast as we could directly at the crick, then with a mighty leap we tried to clear the water to land on the opposite bank. Most times, Gerry's longer legs carried him across. At least half of my attempts landed me in the middle of the crick. However, it didn't matter one least bit. Hey, it was summertime. The hot sun and warm south wind dried my wet pant legs and leather work shoes in a short while. We felt as free as the wind itself.

Life was good. Every so often, a striped gopher whistled sharply as it sat on its haunches near the entrance to its den. Several times, we found trees that had fallen across the crick. These trees invited us to "walk the tight wire"—with arms extended we crossed back and forth on the slippery bark. We examined each hole in the crick to see if the deeper water held any fish.

We were having so much fun that we plumb forgot the reason why we were in the crick pasture in the first place.

Gerry finally asked, "I haven't seen any sign of the horses, have you?"

"Nope, me neither," I replied.

It wasn't more than another hundred yards up the crick where we found fresh horse manure. We hill folk called them horse apples. I pointed at the pile of manure. "Fresh horse apples. They can't be far from here."

We were now in ten acres of country toward the very north end of the crick pasture. Here the crick swung in a wide, sweeping curve against a small hill. Over the course of time, the crick had eaten away at the hill. A great deal of sand and red clay had fallen into the crick bed, which left a high, almost vertical bank. A short way downstream, we found Daisy and Sally on the opposite crick bank in the shade of a giant, spreading-limbed cottonwood tree. The two horses were standing alongside each other, nose to tail so they could help each other out with their fly problems. Old King was not in sight.

Gerry told me to get Daisy and Sally started for home while he went farther up the crick to look for Old King.

I walked over by the two horses and got their minds off their fly problems by stroking each one's forehead and talking to them in an easy, soft way—all the while being careful to watch where my feet were in relation to theirs. One misstep of their huge, round hooves and my poor little foot would be history. I talked to them about going on home with me. I didn't, however, mention anything about makin' hay or going to work.

Soon I had the team moving. Suddenly, they turned sharply and began trotting up the crick. I ran to head them off. I wasn't fast enough; now they were ahead of me. Gerry saw them coming. He began waving his arms and hollering. They went right on by him, turned, and disappeared over a small knoll.

We ran after them. When we got to the top of the knoll, we stopped and stared in disbelief. Daisy and Sally were standing on the crick bank over by the big curve where the hillside had caved into the crick. Old King was standing in the crick facing us. He was up over his belly in mud and water. When we approached, he began to struggle. However, his efforts only sank him deeper into the quagmire.

At first we couldn't speak, couldn't move, didn't know what to do. Then in a very calm voice, Gerry said, "Kenny, you run home as fast as you can. Tell Pa that Old King is stuck in the crick."

"Should I chase Daisy and Sally home ahead of me?" I asked.

"They ain't gonna go home. They ain't gonna leave here without their old pal King. Now you better get started."

I took off as fast as I could. When I got to where the crick narrowed, I took a mighty leap, cleared the water easily, and landed on the bank at a dead run. Across the meadow, down a gully, up the other side I went. When I finally got to the bottom of the hill below the barn, my legs felt like lead, my lungs were on fire, my mouth was dry, and my breath came in short, raspy gulps. Still I ran on up the hill into the barnyard, where Pa was feeding the cows salt and minerals. I stopped alongside him. I was puffing like a steam engine.

"What in Sam Hill's the matter, Kenny?"

"Old King's stuck in the mud in the crick back by the ten acres. I think he's half dead, Pa," I blurted out.

Pa set off at a fast pace across the farmyard. I followed him. In the rickety old machine shed, Pa grabbed a coil of heavy rope, hung it over the back of the seat, and cranked the tractor to life. He backed it out of the shed and told me to climb aboard. I stood on the drawbar and clutched as tight as I could to the seat. We went down the hill on the cattle lane, bounced our way in high gear back to the ten acres country, and pulled to a stop where Gerry was standing by the big curve in the crick.

For a minute or two, Pa just sat on the tractor seat and stared at Old King. He was sunk deeper now than when I had last seen him. Pa's shock soon ended. He got off the tractor and carried the coil of rope to the edge of the crick, where he laid it down. Next, he took one end of the rope and began to wade into the water to Old King. Pa turned and told Gerry to follow him. He hollered for me to hold on to the other end of the rope and to stay put on the bank. When Pa got next to Old King, he began to speak gently to him. Gerry got on the other side of the old horse. The two of them began digging the soft, gooey mud out from beneath the horse's belly in back of his front legs with their hands. Pa then lay down in the muck and shoved the end of the rope under King to Gerry. Gerry brought the rope up and over King's back. Pa then tied a knot and snubbed the rope loop up around the horse.

Pa and Gerry came staggering up the crick bank to where I was standing. There wasn't a square inch on them that wasn't plastered with mud. The three of us dragged the rope up to a level place in the pasture.

Pa backed the tractor over to the end of the rope and tied it to the drawbar. We kids stood aside and watched as the tractor slowly took the slack out of the big hay rope.

Pa was turned sideways in the tractor seat so he could look back at King. When the rope was drawn tight, Pa eased the tractor ahead. The rope stretched, and King moved forward a few feet toward the crick bank. Pa stopped pulling and backed up the tractor while we drew the rope along behind him.

"Old King ain't usin' his legs. We gotta try a different angle," Pa hollered over the noise of the engine.

Again and again we pulled on King with the tractor from different places in the pasture. Each time, King came a little closer to the bank. By now, however, he was lying on his side. He seemed totally unable to move on his own power.

Finally, Pa's tractor pulled King onto dry ground. Still, he did not make any attempt to rise to his feet. He lay quietly in the lush, green grass.

The three of us gathered around him. His eyes looked dull. His breath came and went in short, shallow gasps. There was a long, deep tear in his hide all the way around his belly. Pa knelt to examine it, put his hand on Old King's head, and murmured something I couldn't understand.

Then Pa stood and walked to the tractor. He said, "You boys go down by the old cottonwood next to the crick for a while."

As Gerry and I walked down in that direction, I turned to look back. Pa was getting the single-shot rifle out of its tattered case that hung on the inside of the tractor fender. We stood by the cottonwood tree and watched the water flow by for what seemed like a half a day. The sharp crack of the rifle rang out upon the same gentle summer breeze that sang a soothing lullaby in the cottonwood leaves above us. I covered my ears. Gerry began walking up the knoll. I followed him a ways behind.

When we got there, Old King lay perfectly still in the grass. Pa sat beside him, his head in his hands.

"Why'd we have to kill him, Pa? Why? Why, Pa?" I blubbered.

"'Cause he'd been in the mudhole for a couple of days, fightin' and thrashin' around. He was too old to stand it. And I tore him open pullin' him out. I thought about callin' Doc Speltz, but I knew King was hurt too bad to fix. And he'd of had to wait and suffer. Sometimes, there just ain't no way for a person to turn. He was a wonderful horse. Good in the harness. A darn good friend to boot. Had him twenty-three years. Sure hurts my heart to see him go like this."

As we were coiling up the big rope, Pa said, "I'll tell you one thing. I'm gonna build me a fence around that big curve in the crick so's no other critter ever gits into that blasted old mudhole again. And you kin bet on it!"

Pa drove the tractor home through the crick pasture at a slow pace. Gerry and I followed Daisy and Sally, who were going in the same direction as Pa. They seemed to sense that their old pal wasn't going to travel with them anymore. It was okay to leave him behind.

The frogs and fish and meadowlarks and bluebirds, the gophers and the running, happy waters held no interest for us now. We all just wanted to get home.

Pa phoned up the rendering truck, which picked up dead stock of the large kind. Later that afternoon, he rode along in the truck to pick up Old King. When he got back, he slowly walked over to the gable end of the barn with Ma by his side. The two of them stood there, arms around each other, and stared up at the hay rope dangling from a wooden pulley. Pa kissed Ma on the cheek. She went off to busy herself in the garden. He stood there a while longer. Then he wiped each eye with the back of his hand, turned to us, and said, "Boys, we got us a fence to build over in the ten acres country. Let's go do it!"

And we did.

6. Thrashin' Time

The sun had turned from a bright yellow sphere to a reddish orange ball balanced upon the leafy treetops on the ridges of the nearby western hills. We were in a deep valley, where the evening shadows already stretched long and broad and dusky.

I was shocking grain with my grampa and granny, Adolf and Mary Reglin. Earlier that afternoon, Pa had used a grain binder pulled by Daisy and Sally, our team of horses, to cut down the ripe, golden oats. The binder not only cut the oats, it also securely tied them into bundles with binder twine. The bundles were dropped to the ground every time Pa saw he had enough to make a shock. The magic number was seven.

Now we were walking the field from one pile of bundles to another, putting up shocks. A person would take a bundle in each hand and stand them butt ends on the ground to lean the top ends, which contained the grain, against one another at a sharp angle. This was done three times. Now there were six bundles leaning against each other, three on each side. Then a bundle was placed butt end against one's belly. One arm was held under the bundle. The other hand was used to break the top third of the bundle downward. This bundle was then placed on top of the other six in a horizontal position. It was called a cap, and the shock was complete. The slanted sides covered with a cap made the shock pretty well waterproof, at least for a month or so.

As we walked the field, the fresh-cut grain stubble crunched under our feet. Here and there, a field mouse or a meadow vole scurried out of our way. The pungent smell of fresh-cut oats filled the air and found our noses with the help of the late July breeze. Granny's long work dress swished across the top of the oat stubble like a curtain being dragged over a light straw broom.

After making a complete circle around the field, we stopped by a pile of bundles. Grampa and Granny took a seat on the pile, while I ran back to the first shock to retrieve two tin syrup pails from inside the shock. One pail held water; the other was filled with fresh-baked sugar cookies. I brought the pails to the old folks and took a seat beside them. The cover was removed, and we each took a long, cool drink from the water pail. Then the cookie pail was passed around. Mmm, boy, were they good! Big as your hand, an inch thick, and soft and chewy with sugar sprinkled on top.

All three of us wore big red bandanas. Granny's was tied around her forehead. Grampa and I wore ours around our necks. We all took them off, wrung the sweat out, shook them good and proper, and spread them out on the grain bundles to dry.

By now, the sun had gone to bed. Frogs argued along the banks of the nearby crick. Crickets gossiped back and forth in the field. Whippoorwills repeated their name over and over again in the lowland meadows.

There was little conversation among us shockers. It felt real good to just sit there and rest. We rolled up the long sleeves of our cotton work shirts to allow a better feel of the breeze.

Eventually, the old folks began discussing the merits of this year's oat crop. Granny began: "Adolf, this here stand of oats ain't near what it was when we was a farmin' these here fields. The shocks is farther apart, and the bundles feel lighter to me."

"Well now, Mary, the days when we farmed here was a long spell back," Grampa retorted. "The ground ain't very deep, and every year it gets thinner. Maybe Willard ought to put a little more manure on the ground or plow under some buckwheat or red alfalfa or somethin' like that."

Granny grunted her approval. Then she rolled down her sleeves, reached for her bandana, tied it 'round her head, firmly positioned her battered, wide-brimmed straw hat above it, and stood up. I got myself ready next. Rolling down the long sleeves was the most important task. Exposing one's bare arms to a round of shocking oats would make them look and feel like a pincushion. Shocking rye or wheat or barley was even worse.

Grampa rose last. "Oh, Goot, na, musta," he groaned. I think it meant, "Oh, God, no, musn't," in reference to his aching bones. He reached into his pouch and packed a big gob of Plow Boy chewing tobacco inside his cheek.

Off we went on another shocking trip round the field. On nights when the skies were clear and sister moon shone her gentle light upon the valley, we would work into the early morning hours. Only when our worn leather work boots became soaked with dew would we quit. Even then we did so grudgingly, for though Pa and Gerry and sometimes Ma joined us at night, Pa would be out in the next field come tomorrow running the grain binder. We must keep up with the binder. If a heavy rain came when the bundles lay exposed in the field, it would not be good for the crop. Once the field was shocked, all would be well. Such was the life of a hill country grain shocker.

All of our neighbors were doing the same thing at this time of year. Soon all of the area's fields looked as though thousands of tiny lean-to huts had been built upon the landscape.

After a couple of weeks of curing in the shock, the grain was ready for thrashing. Yes, I know the proper word is "threshing." However, one would never hear that word in the hill country. And after careful reflection upon the event itself, I believe "thrashing" is a more apt description, what with the punishment our bodies endured while performing this task.

It was the most exciting time of the year. It was all about neighbors, about working together for the common good, about helping each other survive in a rugged, tough country. It was about a certain work ethic where every hand, large or small, was valued and praised for its worth to all.

In those days, there were what were called thrashing rings—a rough circle of farmers who thrashed together. In today's words, we pooled our resources. One farmer in the thrashing ring owned the thrashing machine, which he moved from farm to farm until everyone in the ring had their grain in the granary and their straw on the pile. Other ring members provided horses, wagons, forks, shovels, men, women, and children. Also, wherever the machine was working, all food and beverages were provided by that farmer and his wife.

At long last, a week or so after everyone in our thrashing ring was through shocking, it was time to begin thrashing. In our ring, it was Pa who owned and operated the machine, so we started at our place first.

The night before the first day of thrashing, sleep came hard for me. I was so excited. It was like Christmas, Easter, Thanksgiving, and the Fourth of July all rolled up together. Going to the circus wouldn't have been one bit better, as far as I was concerned.

When the first robin sang its promise of a new day, I was up, dressed, and outside. Already somebody was in the yard. Grampa George Salwey had driven out the six miles from Cochrane, where he and Granny Anna lived. He was sitting in his old car with the door open, smoking his pipe. I always marveled at that pipe. The bowl of the pipe was so encrusted with burnt-on tobacco that he couldn't have stuck his little finger into it. In fact, when he took out his can of Prince Albert tobacco, he tamped in only a small, two-fingered pinch. I asked him one time, "Grampa George, why don't you clean your pipe out, so's you can get more into it?"

He grinned. "Why, you little woodchuck, all the flavor'd be gone then. Oh, I scratch it out some once in a while with my jackknife, but not too much. Took me twenty years to get this pipe seasoned just so. Now you want me to ruin it. It ain't how much smoke you get or how long it burns that counts. It's how good it tastes that counts most."

He paused and then added, "You never wanna take it up though. Pipe smokin's a dirty habit if there ever was one. 'Sides that, you'd be sicker'n a grass-eatin' dog to boot, you little woodchuck, you." He laughed.

Today, however, I had other things on my mind besides Grampa George's pipe. I ran over to his car. "Grampa, you ready to start thrashin' today?"

"Reckon I'm as ready as I'll ever be. Where's your pa at?

"Down in the barn choresin', I guess. Want me to go get 'im up here?"

He nodded. I took off for the barn. On the way, I noticed Pa had already pulled the big thrashing machine from its lean-to shed in back of the granary. It was parked a little ways from the barn with the tractor still hitched to it. I got Pa from the barn while Ma and Gerry finished up the milking chores. As we went out the barn door, we passed Daisy and Sally. Both horses were harnessed, resting in their stalls and munching on a little fresh hay. Boy oh boy, everybody was getting an early start this morning.

Now Pa and Grampa George held sort of a meeting: pointing and talking and walking back and forth from the side of the barn to the thrashing machine, then up toward the house a ways.

Finally, Pa started the tractor and moved the machine into position. I helped Grampa put oak blocks on both sides of its big steel wheels. The tractor was unhitched, and Pa drove it toward the house, then turned it to face the thrashing machine about forty feet away. Grampa stood in back of a big pulley on the side of the machine, directing

Pa how to line up the tractor pulley with the one on the machine. When Grampa was satisfied with the position of the tractor, we blocked its tires and the brakes were locked up good and tight.

It took both Pa and Grampa to carry the big drive belt from the tool shed to the tractor. They unrolled the coiled belt from the tractor to the machine. It was about a foot wide and forty feet long. The belt was then put around the machine pulley. One twist was put in it, and the other end was placed around the tractor pulley. The tractor was then backed up to tighten the belt, reblocked, and braked up tight.

Then we went on an inspection tour of the machine. I carried the grease gun and the oil can, which I handed to Pa and Grampa whenever they called for them. Whistling warblers, what a machine it was! It seemed like a great metal monster with a thousand places to grease and oil. A hundred belts and pulleys to check and countless chains and shafts to examine. There was a metal ladder on the back end to climb for working on the top part of the machine. After many trips around and under and over the huge thing, it was pronounced ready to go.

Grampa George started the tractor and slowly let out the clutch, the long belt began to turn, and the monster machine came to life. Belts, pulleys, chains, and shafts worked in unison. Binging and banging, clicking and clattering, grinding and grumbling, rubbing and rattling and roaring. The noise of the great metal gismo was earsplitting. It was an awesome thing to behold. A little at a time, Grampa brought it all to a halt.

Now Pa crawled up on top of the machine. By cranking on what looked like a steering wheel on the end of a small barrel filled with steel cable, he was able to swing a long metal pipe about a foot in diameter out over the cow yard. This pipe was called the blower. Once thrashing began, the stems of the grain, called straw, would be blown out the end of the pipe into the cow yard to form a straw pile. This would be used as bedding for the cattle, horses, and pigs throughout the coming winter. Good fresh, dry straw was a necessity on the farm. Strange as it may seem, even though the straw pile was outside, at the mercy of the elements, if it was constructed properly, the inside would be dry as a bone come spring and beyond.

Pa always tended the blower. The trick to making a good straw pile was to keep it even all around as it went up. No hills and valleys, so to speak. At times, a man or two would spread the straw with forks to make sure it was right.

Pa liked to say, "A good straw pile that's made right'll shed water like it's runnin' off a fat duck's back, that's for sure."

After the thrashing machine was all set, Ma and Gerry came from the barn and we all went into the house for breakfast.

In a short while, Ma served up fried eggs and potatoes done just right in a cast-iron skillet with a quarter inch of hog lard. Thick slices of homemade bread topped with preserved blackberry jam rounded out the morning meal.

As soon as we were through eating, Ma made her voice heard loud and clear. "All right, you guys, up and at 'em. It's time to clear this kitchen of you two-legged workhorses. The women'll be comin' soon. We gotta get cookin' on the dinner, 'cause sure as grass is green, you'll be standin' at the kitchen door like a bunch of hungry bears about twelve noon."

We skedaddled out the door. Grampa George went to his car to "git dressed proper" for thrashin'. I followed him. After digging around in the car trunk, he produced a wide-brimmed straw hat.

"What's that strip of leather that goes round inside your hat, Grampa?" I asked.

"Why, that's called a sweatband, Kenny." He held it out for me to see. "It kinda stops the sweat from runnin' down into my eyes. See this here stain?" His big gnarly forefinger traced a light-brown circle along the top of the sweatband. "That's sweat is what that's from. Soaked clean through the side of the hat from many a summer's worth of wear. Man can sweat just standin' still out here in the month of August. It's enough to melt an iceberg when there ain't no breeze."

"Why ain't I got no sweatband in my straw hat?" I whined.

"'Cause you ain't big enough to sweat good and hard yet, that's why. You're so skinny, might haveta put weights in your pockets on a windy day ta keep you from blowin' away. In time, you'll flesh out some. Then you'll sweat right along with the rest of us, and you'll have you a straw hat with a sweatband in it and a sweat ring, too."

I grinned up at him. He winked at me long and slow and chuckled some. Now he drew a big red bandana from the trunk, tied it about his neck, and took up his wide-necked, homemade hickory cane. We headed toward the tractor.

By now it was about nine o'clock. The morning sun was lifting the dew from the lush summer grass and from the grain shocks in the fields. It was important for the grain bundles to be as dry as possible. If they were damp, they were called "raggy." Raggy bundles pitched into the machine did not thrash well. The grain would not separate from the straw properly. And this was not the only problem with raggy bundles. A plugged-up machine could be the end result. This was bad news, to say the least.

When raggy bundles did make it into the machine, many hours were spent digging, pulling, yanking, twisting, and cutting the plug of wet straw from the machine. Horses had to be taken into the shade. Men sweated and, at times, uttered words not mentionable in mixed company.

Around ten o'clock, the crew began to arrive. They were all dairy farmers, and by then they had half a day's work done already.

Orville Blank was the first to come. He promptly went to the barn, got Daisy and Sally up to the yard, and hitched the team to a flatbed hay wagon. The wagon had a wooden rack on all sides, with the front and back sides higher. Orville was a bundle hauler. Daisy and Sally, for thrashing time, were called a bundle team. A bundle hauler took his team and wagon out into the fields to pick up the grain shocks with a long-handled, three-tined fork. The bundles were not loaded in a pell-mell fashion. They were stacked as flat as possible, butt ends facing out, along the two long sides of the wagon, as far in as the fork would reach. The center of the wagon was filled by tossing bundles into it.

When the situation called for it, a good bundle hauler would come up to a shock, throw the cap in the wagon, and with a mighty lunge stick his fork clean through the shock. This allowed him to load at least four bundles into the center of the wagon at one time. Once in a while, a fork handle bit the dust because of this maneuver. There were, fortunately, always spare forks aboard the wagon.

If the crop was good, the shocks were close together. In that case, the bundle hauler walked alongside the wagon, using long leather straps to guide the team. If the crop was poor, the shocks were far enough apart so that the hauler would jump aboard the wagon to drive the team.

An experienced team of horses knew quite well that they were expected to bring the wagon to a stop alongside each shock. Now and then, one of the horses would reach down to munch a good mouthful of grain off of a shock cap while waiting for the hauler to load the wagon. This "cookie snitching" was tolerated by the hauler as long as it didn't happen too often. A horse could get sick from eating too much grain in a day's time.

The next man in the thrashing ring to arrive was George Fimian. George lived a couple of miles from us across the Waumandee Creek. He had a Western horse as part of his team. The horse was a tawny buckskin color, high-strung and nervous, and sported a genuine bona fide Western brand on its rump. I don't recall how George came into possession of that horse, but it was so much fun to look at. To run my hand over its brand. To wonder where in the great Wild West it had come from and to dream of being a cowboy like the one who had branded the horse. Yessiree, a rootin', tootin', brandin', iron-wieldin', six-gun-totin' cowboy is what I wanted to be.

Oh well, thrashing time in the hill country along the Big River was close enough for now.

Lester Plank farmed a half mile down the hill from us. Some of his land joined ours. I was always welcome there to trap pocket gophers, even though I sometimes made more of a mess of his fields than the gophers did. When he came into the yard, I ran over to him and started talkin' gophers.

Coming in right behind Lester was Pete Blank and his son, Marvin. They lived a mile and a half north in Yeager Valley. Pete was slow and easygoing, smoked a pipe, and always had time to visit with folks. No matter what the weather, time of day, or how much work he had lying ahead of him, Pete never rushed around. He was calm, cool, and collected. Marvin always had a smile at the ready and was quite a jokester. Both he and Pete did a lot of hunting and were great storytellers. They had a black team of horses hitched to their bundle wagon.

Now I stood by the entrance to our driveway, watching up the road to see who else was headed our way. There were two more teams coming. They were, however, quite some distance apart. Big bad buzzin' bees! The guy in the lead was Romey Dittrich, driving his team, Bud and Daisy, both big bay horses with white blazes on their foreheads. He pulled into the driveway, and with a "Whoa now there, Bud," the wagon stopped. I waved my hat at him.

He waved his hat back at me. "Come on up here by your old pal Romey now, Kenny boy."

I jumped up on the wagon wheel, swung myself into the wagon, and stood beside Romey.

"Hup now there, Bud," he said, and away we went. It was an honor to ride into the yard on Romey's rig. He and Grampa George were the oldest working members of our thrashing crew and were well respected by all.

Romey's job was to haul the grain from the thrashing machine to the granary. He had two double-box grain wagons for hauling. A double-box grain wagon had a solid wood box about six feet wide by twenty feet long by four feet high with an end gate that could be removed for unloading. A chain was attached to the middle of the inside of the box with a cinch-type closure. This kept the box from bulging out when loaded.

One of the wagons was parked under the grain spout of the thrashing machine with Bud and Daisy hitched to it. As the wagon box filled, Romey would ask the horses to move the wagon ahead. Rather, I should have said "horse." Almost all of Romey's commands, urgings, shouts, threats, pleadings, and, for that matter, praises were directed at Bud. It was as if Daisy was only there so Romey could say he had a team.

I was there to be Romey's helper. The wagon box always got filled from front to back. It was my job to level off the grain with the top of the box. I always made sure the grain was nice and even in the front. Then a gunny sack was laid on the grain so Romey had a comfortable seat while he managed the horses.

It was amazing how many different things came out of the grain spout besides grain. Grasshoppers, pinch bugs, and about every other kind of insect, including hundreds of crickets, spewed forth from the spout. Most of those were crawling and jumping about. Now and then, a piece of a snake, a frog, or a mouse gave mute testimony to the fact that the insects fared much better on their trip through the thrashing machine.

When the wagon box was full, it was pulled out of the way and replaced with an empty one. I hopped up beside Romey, and we headed for the granary.

Although it was a short ride, the pleasure of it all will never leave me. The smell of the horses, the leather harnesses, and the fresh grain we sat upon. The sound of the squeaks and creaks of a heavily laden wagon with a wheel in need of a little grease. Heavy hooves clopping upon hard-packed, sun-baked ground. The loose end of a chain jingling and jangling in the background. A loud *patoooie* sending a long brown stream of Romey's Plow Boy tobacco juice arching through the air to land with a splat in the hot summer dust.

When we approached the granary, multitudes of English sparrows took flight, along with a few starlings and barn pigeons. They had been cleaning up the spillage around the grain elevator.

The grain elevator was a long metal tube with an auger inside that was mounted on wheels. A hand crank wound cable on a cylinder to raise and lower it. A trough rested on the ground into which the grain was unloaded. The elevator was positioned so that the grain fell into bins in the granary. The elevator was powered by a good-sized electric motor.

Walter Mosiman was the next member of the crew to arrive. He was a bachelor who lived with his mother, Annie, next to the Anchorage schoolhouse up the road a bit where I did my "schoolhousing."

Romey Dittrich's son, Lenny, rounded out the crew. He came into the yard driving his high-spirited team, Sam and Dan, at a trot. Lenny was much like his horses: full of energy, a twinkle in his eye, and a positive attitude. He was always ready for a good laugh.

Now we were ready to start thrashing. The bundle haulers filled their jugs with fresh water and were off to the fields to load up their wagons. Pa rechecked the machine and made sure the blower was set just right to make the straw pile.

Grampa George and Romey talked over the early days of thrashing when a steam engine was used to power the thrashing machine. They discussed the pros and cons of a steam engine versus a tractor. Romey opened up with "One thing about a tractor, you don't have to cut wood to run the consarned thing like you would a steam engine."

"Yah, that's true, Romey," Grampa answered. "But them tractors burn gasoline, and that ain't cheap, and it stinks to boot."

Romey thought a bit. "Know somethin', George? Nothin' in this world's perfect 'cept you and me, and sometimes I wonder about you."

Grampa George made a fist and shook it at Romey. They both laughed.

Grampa climbed up onto the tractor seat, fired it up, and left it to idle. Romey and I walked down by the machine where the grain box wagon was parked. I petted old Bud and Daisy on the nose.

"How come Bud and Daisy's got horsefly netting on 'em?" I asked.

"Well, Kenny boy," Romey replied, "the other horses get to move around a lot, back and forth to the fields, pullin' the wagons from shock to shock and all. The only time they're standin' much is when their wagon's gettin' unloaded at the machine. Bud and Daisy's just the opposite, mostly standin' waitin' for the grain box to fill up. That makes 'em sittin' ducks for horseflies. Them dirty devils kin bite somethin' awful. Now old Bud and Daisy's as steady a team as there ever was, but you never know what a horse'll do if they git bit bad." Romey took a fresh chew of Plow Boy. "Could take to runnin' off. Git wilder 'n a March hare. No stoppin' 'em then." He looked at me close. "More than one person been killed by a runaway team that's been horsefly bit. Snakes is another thing horses ain't real fond of."

George Fimian brought the first wagonload of bundles in along the right side of the thrashing machine. He always unloaded from that side 'cause his Western horse was too skittish around the metal monster machine to come in alongside it close. George wisely kept his horse on the outside, where it would at least tolerate the deafening noise.

Grampa ran the tractor engine at full throttle, the machine began to roar, and George Fimian started to pitch bundles into the yawning maw of the great metal monster. Lenny Dittrich drove Sam and Dan in along the left side of the machine with his load of bundles and began to feed the machine as well.

Dust flew from every opening, no matter how slight, of the machine. Beautiful golden kernels of grain spewed forth from the spout into the double wagon box. And shiny yellow straw shot from the blower into the cow yard. Thrashing had begun in earnest.

Load after load of bundles followed each other through the machine. Pa tended the blower, moving it about to make the straw pile even. Grampa watched the tractor spin the big belt. Romey and I filled the grain box as level as we could.

When the sun was about directly overhead, Ma came out of the house and said something to Grampa. He nodded, and Ma went back into the house. I knew what that meant. Dinner was ready. Jumpin' catfish, I could hardly wait! However, I controlled myself as best I could, 'cause the crew had to all get into the yard before we could eat.

After what seemed like another half a day, the thrashing machine began to wind down. There was a flurry of activity in the yard. Horse teams were unhooked from wagons, led to the metal stock tank for water, and relocated in the shade. Meanwhile, Pa and Grampa George checked over the thrashing machine and the tractor.

Finally, the crew assembled outside the kitchen door. Here there was a wooden washstand that held several large dishpans filled with hot water, a couple of bars of homemade lye soap, and a stack of towels. While some men washed up, others made use of straw brooms to dust each other off.

Dinnertime was not only when the finest of food was served, it was also when a certain amount of good-natured teasing took place. When it came Walter Mosiman's turn to sweep the chaff and dust off Marvin Blank, Walter piped up, "Marvin, I don't know how in the world you could git so wet and dirty at the same time. Sure enough couldn't be from workin' hard and sweatin' and all. What you musta done was poured your water jug over yourself and rolled in the dirt before dinnertime came."

The crew chuckled and offered up comments of their own: "Yah, I was wonderin' the same thing myself. I saw you layin' alongside a shock in the shade this mornin'" and "So that's why you brought in an empty water jug this noon, Marvin."

Marvin laughed loudest of all. "I didn't think you guys would be smart enough to figure out somethin' complicated as that, being most of you are alumni of that little old one-room Anchorage schoolhouse up the road a piece."

At last we all filed into the house for dinner. The delicious smell of true, old-time home-cooking permeated the entire house. A long, wide oak table, already set with place settings, filled the dining room. By the time we were all seated, there were eleven men and one boy waiting at the table to be fed, every one of us hungry as an old bear comin' out of hibernation. We all knew this was gonna be a "sit down and eat till you can't get another forkful of food down your gullet"–type meal of the highest order. That's the way it always was and always would be.

Four women had worked all morning in the kitchen to make sure this was gonna happen. Ma Salwey, Mary Blank, Granny Reglin, and Alethea Blank made up the Fearsome Foursome of Food. All had been born and raised in the hill country. They'd been around the fixing of food and the serving up of it since they were knee-high to a small grasshopper. Their cooking world was filled with recipes that were handed down from one generation to another, some of their own, and even a few from the old country. Each of these ladies was a full-fledged, top-of-the-line cook in her own right.

Cooking was not, however, the only thing they did. No siree, Rudy, they would also *serve* the meal in such a fashion as rarely seen by city folk. Even in the finest of restaurants, one would seldom be so pampered as to have four servers tending hand and foot to a party of twelve. We did, however, have four wonderful servers that day in the old hill country farmhouse.

Huge platters of sliced roast beef garnished with carrots and parsnips were passed around. Next came big bowls of mashed potatoes followed by boats full of rich, smooth, dark-brown gravy. Then there were stacks of thick-sliced, home-baked bread perched on metal trays. Several dishes held a whole pound of butter each. Hot creamed corn made its way around the table. Finally, a couple of bowls of fresh garden lettuce were served without dressing of any kind. Drinks were coffee, Nectar, or fresh water.

The women hovered about the table like mother hens tending to their flock. As soon as a serving dish was half empty, it was taken into the kitchen to be refilled and brought back to the table.

The diners were besieged by offerings from the servers: "More hot taters here for you." "How about roast beef?" "Maybe you'd like some lettuce."

Offerings soon turned to commands: "Take some more corn." "You're gonna have to eat up now. There's lots to come yet." "Don't you pass on that bread. There's two more loaves in the kitchen."

After everybody's second helping of everything on the table, the pleading and begging took place. "Can't you take even a half a slice of bread?" "Please, just a couple a spoonfuls of gravy over a fork or two of beef." "What's the matter, you guys? Are you worried about losin' your girlish figure?"

The final pitch involved reverse psychology seasoned with a good dose of self-pity: "The only reason I can see why you men ain't eatin' like you should today is 'cause you don't like what's on the table. Makes a person feel kinda bad," Alethea mused. Then, for the clincher, she asked, "Don't it make you feel bad, too, Granny?"

Why, I thought to myself, why did Alethea have to ask Granny such a thing? Granny could lay a weight on one's shoulder heavy enough to cause Charles Atlas himself to stagger.

"You know somethin', Alethea, it's a funny thing you should ask. I was just now thinkin' 'bout how I've been cookin' and servin' up meals like the one here on the table for well over fifty years." Granny sniffed up hard and sighed. "I ain't never seen anybody turn up their nose to one of my meals like the people around this table did today." She looked over the top of her glasses at all of us. "Guess I just can't cook like I used to. Might be time to quit."

This was the signal for Ma and Mary and Alethea to begin passing platters and full dishes around the table again.

Talk about being force-fed! We all knew there were delicious pies still to come and had tried to save room for them. Now, under the watchful eye of Granny, we each took another small helping from the passed dishes. All four women nodded and smiled their approval while asking if we were ready for pie now. There was cherry, apple, and lemon to choose from.

After the women felt that the crew was sufficiently stuffed, we were allowed to leave the table. However, before we did, each member of the crew thanked the cooks for the good eats.

Then we all went outside to rest in the shade and let our dinner settle a bit. As we lazed in the grass beneath the big elm trees, a breeze played among the leaves. In the distance, a cicada bug wound up its high-pitched siren over and over again, while barn swallows perched side by side upon the drooping electrical wires, talking over the day's insect hatch.

Now was the time when stories were told and retold. One of them involved me. Somebody said, "Say, Romey, ain't you gonna take Kenny down to the barn and have him show you what kinda bull his pa's got in there?"

Laughter rippled through the crew. From behind the trunk of one of the big elms came, "Yah, Romey, we think it's time Kenny gits reminded of the spellin' lesson you gave him a while back." Knowing glances were directed at both Romey and me.

Romey packed a golf-ball-sized wad of Plow Boy in his left cheek, spat once, and cleared his throat. "Well, you see, fellas, it was like this. About two years ago on a day pretty much like this, we come outta the house after dinner. Was gonna sit in the shade here a spell. Kenny boy says to me, 'Pa got us a new bull. Wanna take a look at 'im?'

"I said I would, so we ambles down to the barn over yonder, gits inside, walk over to the bull pen. There stands a dandy young bull, maybe twelve hundred pounds or so. Nice slick-lookin' thing he was.

"I says, 'Kenny boy, what kinda bull you got there,' just to see if the kid knew his cattle. He says, 'It's a Guernsey.' I stood and pondered that for a while. Then I mentioned how I thought that bull had a little red pole in him. Kenny piped right up and told me his bull didn't have no Red Poll breed of cattle in him at all. I stared into the bullpen a minute or two and said I now knew for sure he had a little red pole in him.

"Kenny boy not only took the bait, he swallowed it hook, line, and sinker. He hollered out, 'Romey, look at 'im close. He got no Red Poll in 'im. You can see he's a Guernsey.'

"Poor boy was gittin' all riled up over the whole thing, so I decided to let 'im off the hook. I allowed as how it was him who wasn't lookin' close enough and he should look under that bull's belly towards the back end and he'd see some of that little red pole the bull had in 'im.

"The kid did and stood there shakin' his head. Couldn't help myself, had to chuckle a little bit. I went over to 'im, put my hand on his shoulder, looked down at 'im and I says, 'Kenny boy, hope I didn't hurt your feelins none. See, this old hill country billy goat never put his foot in a schoolhouse a whole lot. Yet it ain't always books that teaches lessons. There's a lesson in this bull thing here. It's about words. See, two words kin be said the same but not spelt the same. And they kin mean somethin' as different from each other as day from night. Now ain't you glad, Kenny boy, it was old Romey taught you that rather'n Harriet Hogan up the road there in that little ole schoolhouse?' He looked up at me and smiled, and we was pals again. Still are, ain't we, Kenny boy?"

I nodded my head, and the whole crew nodded theirs in full approval as well. Eventually, the crew arose with assorted murmurs, grunts, and groans, and everyone headed back to the work at hand. Bundle haulers drove their teams out to the fields to load up shocks. Brother Gerry went with them to be a "field pitcher," which means he roamed the field from one wagon to another, pitching bundles aboard wherever needed. Grampa George climbed onto the tractor. Pa crawled on top of the thrashing machine to tend the straw blower, and Romey and I headed for the grain wagon. And so i t went through the long, hot afternoon. Load after load of bundles were pitched into the machine. Straw flew from the blower, and grain ran heavy into the grain box wagon.

Every time we hauled a load to the granary, I was amazed to watch Romey back his faithful old team and wagon into such tight quarters—and he made it look easy, to boot. He always stood on the ground alongside the wagon instead of sitting on the front looking backward. As he liked to say, "I kin see the whole picture at once this way."

Despite his years, Romey stood as straight as a rifle barrel. Tall and lean as a whip. Straw hat canted a little to one side of his head. His weathered face seemed to lean some as well, due to the Plow Boy bulge in his left cheek. A blue cotton shirt, buttoned tight at the neck and cuffs, was tucked inside a pair of bib overalls, which were rolled up to expose well-worn, twelve-inch-high leather work boots. Long leather driving lines were loosely held in his calloused hands, the ends trailing behind him in the dirt.

"Back up, Bud." Romey barked out his directions like a drill sergeant, and the horses began to move. The slightest pressure from the lines usually brought an instant reaction from the horses. However, if it didn't, he would plead, "C'mon, Bud, over this way now, will you?" When things were going the way they should, he was lavish with praise: "That's it. That's the way. Good boy, Bud."

The wagon eased into position for unloading. When the end gate touched the elevator, it did it so gently that one could have held a finger in between and hardly felt any pressure. More than once, I thought about doing just that. Common sense did, however, prevail.

Next the elevator was turned on, the end gate was removed, and "we" began to unload. I say we only in the sense that I was there to watch Romey use a scoop shovel to push the grain into the elevator. The bottom of the grain box wagon was lined with smooth, flat tin, making it easier to slide the grain to the back of the wagon.

Romey liked to recall the old days when, as he said, "There weren't no such things as elevators. We put the grain in big, tall canvas sacks, tied 'em shut, and carried 'em on our shoulders into the granary up the steps and dumped 'em in the grain bin. Weren't too hard to sleep that night. Just fall into bed and start snorin'."

When the grain wagon was empty, the four of us—Bud, Daisy, Romey, and I—would plod our way back to the thrashing machine.

Since we had left the house after dinner, the Fearsome Foursome of Food had eaten their own dinner, washed all the dishes, and prepared supper. About five-thirty in the evening, the thrashing operation shut down for a while, and another huge meal was presented to us. Pork chops rubbed with thyme and smothered in applesauce. Fried potatoes and onions. Fresh bread and butter and strawberry preserves. Green beans with bacon mixed in. And, of course, homemade pies.

During the meal, the topic of eatin' habits came up. Lenny Dittrich mentioned how he'd read a article in the paper: "Folks gonna have to watch their calories 'cause they're gettin' too fat for their own good."

Grampa George wanted to know what in Sam Hill a calorie was. A couple of the younger men explained it to Grampa as best they could. He took it under consideration and allowed as how it was no wonder to him that folks was roundin' themselves out in all directions.

"Hey, instead of pumping water by hand or dippin' it from a spring, they turn on a faucet," he said. "'Stead of choppin' wood, they twist a dial an' they got heat. They ride around in cars and tractors and such, 'stead of walkin'. Next thing you know, they'll be jumpin' around and runnin' up and down them roads they're buildin' all over now' days. All of 'em tryin' to kill them blasted calalees. Tell you what, fellas. Why don't them folks come on out here in the hills and help us make wood and butcher hogs and thrash grain? No time at all, they'd see them calalees they're so scared of drippin' off the end of their nose in the shape of good, honest, hardworkin' sweat. I don't think it's so much the calalees that's the problem. The trouble might lie in all the restin' what's done in between eatin'."

He added, "Look around this table. Nobody here is roundin' themselves out, and look at what we all eat. Like hogs at a trough we are."

As soon as the women were reasonably sure everyone in the dining room was stuffed to the gills with fine food, they released us.

There was, however, no dallying in the shade now. About half the crew headed out for their farms to do the evening milking and other chores. Those who stayed had wives, older children, or hired men at home who could take care of things.

For the other half of the crew, the thrashing routine began again. While we were waiting for the grain box wagon to fill, I asked Romey why we called the work we were doing thrashing.

"Humph," he grunted. "Pretty simple. The bundles go into the machine and git thrashed around and cut up some. Then they git thrashed some more somethin' awful in there, till the grain is thrashed plumb offa the straw. Some say it's called threshin'. Don't know where that come from, and I don't care, either. We call it thrashin'. That's always been close enough for me."

About an hour before dark, all thrashing activities stopped for the day. The evening dew was beginning to settle into the valley fields, which made the bundles too raggy to thrash. There was much cleaning up to be done around the machine and down by the granary. All pitched in to help.

Then, one by one, they left for home and a well-deserved night's rest. Tomorrow would mean another day of thrashing. Soon our fields would be finished. Then the machine and the crew would move to a neighbor's farm and then to another until all the members of the crew had their straw piles built and their grain safely stored in the granary.

Romey was the last to leave. I followed his grain wagon to the end of our driveway.

"Whoa now, Bud," he drawled. "See you in the mornin', Kenny boy. Sleep tight. Don't let the bedbugs bite. Hup now, Bud."

"See you, Romey pal," I cried out. "See you, Bud. See you, Daisy." I watched them go until I could see them no more; however, I could still hear the jangle of harness chains and the clip clop of hooves as they kept time to the lovely birds' songs as they said goodnight to one another.

Tomorrow would be another good day.

I just knew it would.

7. Granny and Grampa

"It's a fish day," said Granny. She stood in front of the calendar hanging on the kitchen wall near the pantry. "You go on out and get your Grampa up off of the porch couch and get to diggin' some worms for us."

"Yippee!" I hollered. I jumped up and down, then took off running for the porch door to roust Grampa from his noontime nap.

Grampa and I walked across the farmyard to the tool shed where I selected a five-tined manure fork as a diggin' tool and picked up a two-pound coffee can to hold the worms.

Under the shade of a big elm tree at the edge of the garden, Grampa turned over forkfuls of ground while I picked up nice, fat, wriggly worms to put in the can along with some ground.

"Diggin' worms is one of the best parts of goin' fishin', ain't it, Grampa?" I asked.

"It sure is, Boobily," he answered. "It's good to get your own bait for fishin'. Nowadays, some folks go and buy it." He shook his head.

We walked over to the garage, which was actually a lean-to off the side of the granary. He swung the big hinged door open and told me to get back out of the way of the car and to stay there. He needn't have worried. Anytime Grampa was behind the wheel of that car, anybody with a lick of sense stayed out of his way. Let's just say that Grampa would not have been counted among the world's best drivers.

I heard the car door slam, and Grampa fired her up. A moment or two later, the rear end of the battered old Chevy appeared in the open garage doorway amid a cloud of bluish smoke. Through the open car window, he yelled for me to go tell Granny we were ready to go.

However, Granny was already coming across the yard. She wore a wide-brimmed straw hat that had a leather strap under her chin. A long-sleeved cotton shirt fit over a dress that reached to about a foot off the ground. Her apron was just a little shorter than the dress. On her feet, she wore leather shoes inside of four-buckle rubber galoshes. In one hand, she carried a handmade picnic basket; in the other, she gripped a worn old walking cane. She walked with a slight limp, which caused one footfall to sound a little louder than the other.

A smile creased her weathered face. "You got lots of big fat worms dug?"

"Yup, we got tons of 'em." I glanced at her basket and said, "Is our lunch in there, Granny?"

"Sure is. Along with a big jug of fresh-pumped water." She added, "I reckon we're ready to head for the crick."

Meanwhile, Grampa was examining the fishing gear. Three cane poles leaned against the side of the car. Two of the poles were longer than the car itself; the other one was perhaps a few feet shorter. Tied to the business end of each pole was a length of black braided line that ended a foot short of the butt end of the pole. A long, shanked hook was tied to this end of the line with a heavy lead sinker clamped six or eight inches above the hook. On one of the long poles' lines, a brown piece of cork the size of a tennis ball was fastened with a white cord wrapped around it to keep it from slipping off the line. This was Granny's pole.

She always said, "There ain't no person in their right mind who'd go fishin' without a cork on their line. If there ain't no cork to go under the water, how'd you ever know you had a bite?" We never argued the point.

Granny got into the old Chevy on the passenger side. I sat in the middle of the front seat. We waited there while Grampa tied the cane poles lengthways to the outside door handles on the passenger side. The poles stuck out so far in back that he had to tie his red handkerchief to them for safety reasons.

He got into the driver's seat, turned the key, and the old Chevy came to life. Now, Grampa had never really made a smooth transition from horses to the gasoline engine. His right foot pushed down hard on the gas pedal. His left foot slowly let up on the clutch. As the car slowly began to move forward, he held the clutch halfway in and halfway out, thereby producing a herky-jerky, jumping, thrusting forward motion, while a blue-gray cloud of smoke bellowed from the tailpipe.

Granny clutched the window crank with one hand and braced herself against the dash with the other hand. Her teeth were clenched.

My feet were pushed firmly against the floorboards, while my elbows were locked under the armpits of Granny and Grampa on either side of me.

Grampa stared straight ahead with a white-knuckled grip on the steering wheel. We were ready for takeoff. We coughed, smoked, jumped, and thrust our way down the driveway to the main road, where we took a right-hand turn.

Sometimes we would turn into Ed and Lydia Plank's farm a short distance down the road. We'd rumble across their oak-plank bridge, park the car in their pasture, and fish where Yeager Valley Crick joined the Waumandee Crick. At other times, we would continue down the main road to the site of an old Civilian Conservation Corps (CCC) camp. Here a great stone chimney stood in a lowland cow pasture, a stone's throw from the Waumandee Crick. This land belonged to a widow named Julia Suhr.

Today, however, we went on a much longer trip. An old friend of Grampa's, name of Gus Fleckiesen, lived on a small farm overlooking the Waumandee Crick two miles downstream of the CCC camp.

Grampa brought the old Chevy to a lurching halt alongside of Gus Fleckiesen's pasture fence.

We unloaded the fishin' stuff and Grampa headed for his favorite hole: a sharp curve just upstream from a wood-plank bridge.

I stuck with Granny. She usually caught the most fish. We crossed a hundred yards of pasture to sit beside a slow pool shaded by the spreading limbs of an ancient silver maple.

At this place, the Waumandee Crick was actually a small river consisting of half a dozen hill country cricks. The waters ran deep and easy.

Granny dug her reading glasses from her apron pocket, brought her fish hook up to eye level, pursed her lips, and proceeded to thread a couple of nice, fat worms onto the hook.

Next, she took a firm, two-handed grip on her cane pole and swung the line, big cork, sinker, and hook full of wiggling worms directly to her rear. She rested the pole on her shoulder and looked straight ahead at the water. It was as if she were gathering up all the strength she could muster for the forthcoming cast.

With a loud grunt, she'd whip the monstrous pole forward and send the fishing line and everything attached in a high, whistling arc through the air, to land with a *kaploosh* in the deep water before her.

She nodded her approval as to the accuracy of the cast and bent to jam the butt end of the pole into the soft crick bank at her feet. The giant pole hung quietly out over the water, waiting for action to develop.

Granny plopped a five-gallon metal pail upside down on the bank, placed her cornhusk-stuffed pillow on it, and took a seat. She adjusted her dress for comfort, tilted her straw hat for just the right amount of shade, and settled back to begin her vigil.

There would be no fidgeting about, little or no talking, the pole would not be raised to see if the worms were in good shape, absolutely no dozing, and you could bet your life she wasn't about to move up- or downstream to find a better fishing hole. No siree, Bob. Granny was set up for the duration.

Many's the time when talking fishing she would observe, "One word means the most when you're fishin'. Patience. You got to have patience. Fish ain't a whole lot different from us. If you just finished a big meal and somebody come along and dropped a pork chop on the table, you wouldn't be about to eat it, would you?" She continued, "You'd probably go off and rest a spell. Later on, after three, four hours, you might wanna come back to the table lookin' for that pork chop. But it ain't there no more, so you can't grab for it. Same way with fishin'. The worms is got to stay on the table at all times."

There weren't a whole lot of people who argued with Granny's reasoning. It's just that most folks did not possess patience to that degree, especially a scrawny little six-year-old like me.

I baited my hook with a big gob of worms, swung my line out into the water, stuck the butt end of my pole into the bank, and sat down on the grassy bank to wait for a bite.

Off to my side, Granny murmured, "Fishin' corkless again, huh?" I turned in time to see her shake her head in disgust.

During the next hour or so, I fidgeted about, checked my bait a half-dozen times, and made several short trips up and down the crick to look for better fishing holes.

As I was returning from one of these jaunts, I saw Granny standing up and doing battle with a fish. I ran to the edge of the crick. Granny pulled her long pole toward her. Hand over hand it slid on the bank in back of her. As the fish began to tire, she pulled it closer to her.

When the fish slipped into the shallow water near the bank, I grabbed the black braided line and hauled a flopping two- to three-pound catfish out of the water and swung it to the top of the bank.

By the time I'd scrambled up there, Granny had her foot on the fish and a pliers in its mouth. She quickly removed the hook.

I knew the drill. I went to her pail, got a burlap bag—what we called a gunnysack—out of it, and went to pick up the fish from under her foot.

"Careful now," she said. "Look out for them two spines in back of the gills and the one on the top fin, too, or you'll get horned and that ain't no fun."

I slid my hand under the fish, gripped it as tight as I could, and laid it in the gunnysack. Then I took the sack down to the edge of the water, along with a two-foot-long stick I found lying under our shade tree. Next, I pinned the open end of the sack into the bank with the stick and tossed the other end, which held the fish, into the crick. I climbed to the top of the bank in time to hear Granny say, "Look out, Kenny, I'm casting now." The big pole whooshed, the line whistled, and her bait hit the water with a mighty splash.

The rest of the afternoon slipped by in pretty much the same way. Every so often, Granny would hook a fish, I'd help her land it, she'd unhook it, and I'd put the fish into the sack soaking in the crick.

However, for a short while, Granny had "rat trouble." A muskrat swam close by her big cork and disappeared around the upstream bend. Soon, it would come paddling down carrying a mouthful of grass that trailed in the water alongside it. The rat then dove under the opposite bank, only to reappear and do the whole thing over again.

Once Granny clapped her hands at the swimming rat. It paid no attention at all.

"That rat's using the grass to fix her up a nest and to feed her babies. She's just bein' a good momma, that's all." Granny smiled and chuckled a bit. "She might scare a fish or two away, but what of it? She's got a family to feed, and we already got our supper caught, so go 'head and swim through my fishin' hole, you little old rat."

A while later, we saw Grampa trudging across the pasture toward the car. It was time to go home. Granny and I gathered up our gear and headed for the car as well.

At the car, the picnic basket was opened. The three of us sat on the long, wide running board of the old Chevy while we devoured smoked summer sausage sandwiched between slices of buttered homemade bread. The glass water jug was unwrapped from a towel and passed back and forth until our thirst was quenched. The fishing tools were loaded and we chugged up the road for home.

Back at their little farm, Granny and Grampa put a huge metal washtub under the hand-operated water pump that stood just outside the north porch door. The burlap fish sacks were emptied into the washtub. Oh, this was the most exciting part of the whole day—counting and sorting and looking at the fish!

Grampa told me to "pump that tub plump full of water so's the fish stay fresh" as he went off to do some farm chores.

I carefully began to sort the fish. There were five crick suckers, three carp, and four catfish. Holy mackerel! Twelve fish in one afternoon! I wished I would have caught one. Oh, well, maybe next time. I could hardly wait.

Now to pump the water. Grampa had once explained to me that the leathers in the pump were worn, so there was always a half pail of water standing nearby to prime the pump.

The water was poured from the pail into the top of the pump. Then the four-foot-long pump handle was pumped up and down with smooth, slow strokes. At first, water trickled from the spout. Each stroke produced more, until great gushes of cool, clear water fell into the waiting washtub full of fish below.

After the fish were covered with water, I went into the house to help Granny carry out the butchering tools. There were several long-bladed, razor-sharp butcher knives, a couple of two-foot-square cutting boards, a number of enameled dishpans, some scaling spoons, wiping rags, and a cleaver the size of which you could have used to fell a small tree.

The tools were all taken to the fish bench—a rickety old knife-scarred wooden table that leaned against the side of the woodshed a short distance from the house. Here we set up shop.

By now, Grampa was back from doing the evening chores. The fish cleaning began shortly. It was my job to take a pail over to the washtub, pick out a couple of fish, and deliver them to Grampa and Granny, who stood ready at the fish bench.

The suckers were first. I dumped them on the table, two at a time. Each was laid on a cutting board where my grandfolks would grip them by the head with one hand while holding an old tablespoon in the other. Beginning at the tail, the spoon was scraped against the grain of the scales, which caused the loosened scales to fly in every direction. Once the fish was free of scales, Grampa lopped the head and tail off with the long, wood-handled cleaver. The insides were removed and the whole works was dropped into a five-gallon metal slop pail. I then took the butchered fish to the water pump in a dishpan to scrub and clean it with a small brush.

The carp went to the table next. The scaling process was done with a butcher knife. The scales were cut off from tail to head. Again, the head and tail were removed. Then the cleaver was used to split the carp lengthways along the backbone.

By this time, every cat on the farm had followed its nose to the fish bench. There was much meowing, muttering, and munching going on. Most of the muttering was of the human kind. Cats were everywhere underfoot, milling about, fighting over every scrap and morsel they could find. Some tried to climb up the table legs and, at times, the people legs as well.

Granny showed her usual endless patience by merely brushing and shoving the cats aside.

Grampa, however, grabbed a few fish heads from the slop pail, threw them inside the open woodshed door, and began herding the whole bunch of cats through the door.

He shouted, "Roust mit der kutz," plus a few other German phrases that I did not understand; however, the cats seemed to. He slammed the door behind them.

Back at the fish bench, Granny said a few rather sharp words in German to Grampa and they both went back to the work at hand.

The catfish were the last to be cleaned. A half-inch-deep cut was made in back of the gills all around the fish. A pliers was used to grip the skin and work it slowly, one side and then the other, always pulling from head to tail until the fish was cleanly skinned. Like the others, it was then gutted, head and tail removed, scrubbed, washed, and put in a dishpan of water. The fish "butchering" was finished.

Now the dishpans full of fish were carried into the house, down the steep basement steps, and put in the root cellar, where it was always cool and dark, for overnight keeping.

The next day, Granny and Grampa would cut up all of the suckers and most of the carp into two-inch-square pieces for pickling. The smallest carp and every catfish would be saved for savory meals of fresh, fried fish for several days to come.

In the meantime, I said goodbye to Granny and followed Grampa across the farmyard to the chicken pen, where the slop pail full of fish cleanings was dumped inside the woven-wire fence. The flock of chickens came running from all corners of the pen and picked and scratched at their unexpected evening meal.

"You be careful now, Boobily," Grampa said as he patted the top of my head. "Granny'll have fish cooked for dinner. Tomorrow noon, come on down."

I said I would as I started across the hayshed meadow toward home. Our cow dog, Rover, and little Brownie met me halfway up the hill to walk me home in the long shadows of dusk.

That night I dreamt in peaceful sleep of wriggling worms, quiet waters, fishing poles, flopping fish, and clamoring cats.

That day took place over sixty years ago. However, there would be countless others spent over the next three decades with my maternal grandparents—true old-time hill folk they were. So come on along. Let's go visit Grampa and Granny Reglin in a time when life was slower and simpler. They'll be mighty happy to get to know you.

Grampa was born in the spring of 1881 to German settlers, near the sleepy little hill country village of Cream, Wisconsin, as the crow flies maybe six miles east of the Mississippi River. His name was Adolf Reglin. He was born and raised and lived and died in Buffalo County, Wisconsin. I don't think he ever traveled more than fifty miles from home.

Granny was born to Swiss settlers in the summer of 1885 near a country crossroad general store and saloon in a place called Tell, Wisconsin. Her name was Mary Kindschy. At the age of ten, she and her family moved twelve miles south and a little east to the lower Waumandee Valley.

Adolf and Mary met in their teen years. A romance developed, and in November of the year 1902, they were married.

They farmed among the hills where Yeager Valley joins the lower Waumandee Valley. When they sold the farm, they kept twenty-eight acres for their "retirement farm" just down the hill and across the crick from where they had raised their family.

It is here in the big, rambling, square farmhouse with its wraparound porch, the little barn, the chicken coop, the granary, the woodshed, the garden, and across the entire farmyard where we shall hear their voices once again. Together, we will practice the old ways, follow the ancient trails, and experience the joys and the hardships of a simple life lived close to the land.

Going pickin' was one of my favorite things to do with the old folks. The hill country produced an endless variety of things to pick and gather, depending on the time of the year and what your taste took a fancy to.

With the coming of spring, the green things began to poke their heads from the earth. At first they were afraid, for the nights were still frosty. However, with each passing day, the sun climbed higher, the breezes turned to the south, and gentle April showers fell.

This was about the time when Granny would announce, "It's time to do a little plantin', so we can do a little pickin' later."

It was time to spade the garden, which ran along two sides of the house. To spade meant to turn over the ground with a long-handled, broad, flat-bladed tool.

Grampa did the spading, while I followed behind with a coffee can, competing with a few brave robins for nice, fat worms. The smell of the fresh spring earth lingered in the air.

Then an old, heavy steel rake was used to smooth the ground for planting. I'd run in to tell Granny it was ready. She would declare, "The taters are always first planted."

Oh, how I loved to plant taters! We'd go down in the basement to the root cellar. Here there was a tater bin made of wood planks, about six feet square and two feet deep. The potatoes left over from winter's supply were sprouted; small thin stems, as many as four or five to each potato, had emerged. We put the potatoes into pails and took them upstairs to the kitchen table, where we each had a cutting board and a sharp knife.

"Now," Grampa would say, "we're gonna make little ones out of big ones."

The potatoes were cut into chunks. Each chunk had at least one sprout on it. These chunks were called seed taters and were taken to the garden in a large pail.

Grampa dug small holes, maybe six inches deep and two feet apart, in a straight line to form a row.

Granny and I would place a seed tater in each hole, cover it with ground, and move to the next hole.

"Them sprouts are called the 'eyes' of the seed tater," Granny would remind me, "and they got to be facing up or that poor old tater won't know which way to grow." She'd wink at me and we'd go on planting.

When April showers brought forth the May flowers and the first lilacs bloomed, it was time to go picking morel mushrooms and wild asparagus. Certain gear was needed for this task. First, a good stout walking stick about twice as big around as your thumb was cut from an ash sapling. When standing upright, the stick should reach to the top of your shoulder. All branches were clipped off flush with the stick using a small hand axe. The bark was stripped and the stick allowed to dry in a cool, dark place. If the stick was dried in the sun, it would most likely twist and warp, causing it to be as "crooked as a walked-on snake," as Grampa used to say.

Why a walking stick?

It's a third leg going up or down a hill. It's balance when crossing a log. It tests the depth of water or mud. It picks up or moves things out of the way, like small branches, long grass, or maybe a snake or two. The most rewarding use, however, is when you lean on it with both hands, pull it against your chest, and simply stand there to rest a spell. Perhaps you want to enjoy a view or think about something for a while. So a walking stick not only enables one to walk with greater ease, it enables one to stop walking with greater ease as well. Seems to me that's important. You're not so likely to miss out on so many things that way.

The next thing needed would be a shoulder bag. We usually made these out of a hundred-pound burlap bag or, as the old folks called them, gunnysacks. The sack was folded or rolled, top half inside of the bottom half; now the sack was of double thickness and ready for the shoulder strap, which would go over your head, around the top of the shoulder, and down under the opposite arm. Here it would be attached at two corners of the open end of the sack.

Shoulder straps varied in size according to the person and in makeup according to whatever material was available. A leather or canvas strap was top-of-the-line. It could be fastened to the sack by hand-sewing with braided fishing line or some sort of cord string.

However, for most hill folk in those days, the most readily available strap material was plain old hemp rope or, in later years, twine string. The problem with either of those was that when carrying a heavy load, the strap would cut into one's shoulder. This was solved by affixing a piece of gunnysack to the rope strap where it rode upon the top of the shoulder.

Grampa's admonition was, "If you carry on like you're a contortionist"—the largest English word I ever heard him speak—"when you're puttin' on your shoulder bag, quit and make you a new one. Life'll go a lot better for you."

A shoulder bag was sometimes worn for eight, ten, or even twelve hours, so comfort was important. The bag was worn to carry whatever we might pick; however, it also served as a "possible bag." Anything we might possibly need for the day—a water jug, toilet paper, a knife, sandwiches—all went into the bag.

Shortly after the early morning dew had risen from the lush springtime grasses, we walked single file from the farmyard up into the nearby forested hills.

I was the "bird dog" for our trio. When a dead or dying elm tree was spotted, I would go to it to see if any morel mushrooms grew there. Meanwhile, the old folks would lean on their walking sticks or sit on a downed log to await my report. If I found mushrooms, they would join me for the picking. There were two colors to the morels: gray and yellow, with the yellow being the largest. Using my thumb and forefinger, I'd pull the mushroom from the ground. A knife was used to cut off the bottom inch of the stem, removing any ground from the mushroom. One of Granny's old pillowcases was pulled from a shoulder bag to hold the mushrooms. I loved to look at the spongelike texture of the Christmas tree–shaped morels and to sniff their burnt almond odor.

So the morning went, walking from one elm tree to another—some had mushrooms under and around them, some did not—looking, searching. and poking. I felt like an old-time gold prospector. Along the way, many plants, shrubs, and trees were examined. I had many questions, which Grampa and Granny patiently took the time to answer.

A white-flowered bloodroot plant was dug. I was allowed to break the root. As the red juice dribbled across my fingers, I exclaimed, "It's bleeding! It's bleeding!"

They both chuckled. "That's why it's called blood-root, Boobily."

The small blue-purple violets that stood proudly shimmering in the springtime sun could be used to make a tasty tea.

Stinging nettles, if picked when less than a foot high, made a pretty good steamed vegetable.

Various trees were identified and discussed. The shagbark hickory we would revisit come early fall to gather its nuts. The acorns of the red, black, and white oak trees would be gathered by squirrels, chipmunks, deer, turkeys, and other folks of the forest. Gooseberry, elderberry, blackcap, and blackberry patches were noted and committed to memory for future pickin' trips. Everywhere we went, there were new things to see, to learn about, to ponder, and to wonder about and absorb.

Finally, Granny looked to the sky, shaded her eyes with her hand, and uttered a single, wonderful word: "Dinnertime."

All three of us sat on a fallen tree trunk. We took sandwiches of dried summer sausage, cheese, and home-baked bread from our shoulder bags and washed them down with long, deep pulls out of the water jugs.

From our hillside vantage point, the Waumandee Crick looked like a narrow blue ribbon winding its way among small ponds filled with sparkling gems in the valley far below.

While we ate, Granny waxed philosophical: "You know, us hill folk eat an early breakfast: some kind of meat and taters and homemade bread with a berry jam spread on it. At noon, we have dinner. Maybe two-thirty or three o'clock, we'll lunch a little—a couple cookies, some coffee or such. About five-thirty, six o'clock, we eat supper, a full meal just like we do at noon." She looked at Grampa and me to see if we were listening, then went on.

"A while back, some city folk friends of ours gave us an invite to their place for Sunday dinner at Winona, Minnesota. On Sunday morning, a while after breakfast, we drove the old Chevy on down there. Boobily, you know what it's like to ride all of thirty miles in the old Chevy with your grampa drivin'."

I sat motionless. My eyes didn't even twitch, 'cause I knew Grampa was watching me.

Granny continued. "Well, when we got there a little before noon, our friends was surprised to see us. They said we was over six hours ahead of time, that dinner would be served about six o'clock that night. We felt whole foolish.

"They told us our 'dinner' was their 'lunch' and their 'dinner' was our 'supper' and we all laughed. Then they rustled us up some dinner/lunch—whatever it's called—but it sure was good, wasn't it, Adolf?"

Grampa nodded his head. "Yup, yeah, times are a changin'."

We shouldered our bags, took up our walking sticks, and made our way down the hill to a one-car-wide gravel road. The road led us into a long, deep, narrow valley. Here and there along the grassy roadside banks, we found wild asparagus plants. The tall dead stalks from last year tipped us off as to where the new plants were. Among the dead stalks, finger-sized, six-inch-high green shoots stood. These were harvested with a knife and placed in a clean pillowcase to ride their way home in our shoulder bags.

Back at the old folks' farm, the asparagus shoots were cut into bite-sized pieces and the mushrooms were split lengthways. Everything was then washed and left to soak in a dishpan full of cold water.

As spring slid into summer, there was always plenty to do. Each morning, there were five cows to be milked by hand. These were Holstein, Guernsey, and Brown Swiss cows. One cow wore a bell that hung from a leather strap around her neck. When the cows were in the pasture, the tinkle of the bell told their location. Most mornings, the cows would be waiting close to the barn for milking time. Grampa would open the barn door and call, "Come, Bos. Come, Bos. Come on in." Each cow knew which stall was hers and promptly went into it. In front of each stall was a manger, which held some freshly ground corn and grain. While the cows ate their breakfast, Grampa took turns going in alongside each cow to sit on his little milk stool. He held the pail between his knees and hand-squeezed the milk from the cow's udder.

After milking, the cows were turned out to pasture until evening, when the entire process was repeated.

There was a little eight-foot-square lean-to on the barn called the milk house. Here there were a couple of metal milk cans. A strainer was placed in a can, and the milk from the pail was poured through the strainer into the three-foot-high, double-handled milk can. The can was then placed in cold water. Every couple of days, the milk hauler would stop by with a flatbed truck to pick up the full cans and leave empty ones in the milk house.

There was a small wooden corner cupboard in the milk house that held something of great interest to me and Grampa alike. On the middle shelf stood a large can of Plow Boy Chewing Tobacco. At times, I'd follow Grampa into the milk house and watch him take the can down, reach in there, and come out with a three-fingered gob of chewing tobacco. He'd tuck that in between his cheek and gum on the left side of his mouth, work it around a little, go outside, and spit a long, brown stream of tobacco juice onto the ground. Once in a great while, I'd ask him, "Grampa, kin I have a little taste out of that can?"

The answer was always the same: "Nix, nix, Boobily. You got to grow up awhile yet before you take some of that stuff." The very reason I only asked him once in a great while was 'cause I figured I might have grown up enough in the while since I last asked. Oh, well, maybe next time. And off we'd go to do other things.

One day as I walked from my parents' farm on the hilltop overlooking Granny and Grampa's place, I could hear the ring of Grampa's axe. He was makin' firewood for the next winter in the woods above his barn. After I'd crossed the crick, I saw Granny weeding in the garden. The thought of that forbidden can of Plow Boy standing in the milk house cupboard with nobody near it struck my mind. In a few minutes, there was somebody near it all right: me! I eased the cupboard door open, took the can from the shelf, brought a three-fingered gob out of it, and put it between my cheek and gum on the left side of my mouth. Now I worked it around some, went outside, and spit a long, brown stream of tobacco juice onto the ground. Then I went in back of the barn to do my chewing in private. I sat down on a chunk of limestone in the shade of the barn roof and did a fair amount of chewing. A problem was starting to take shape. The more I chewed, the more juice I found in my mouth. Grampa, however, only spit once as far as I ever knew, so I swallowed as much juice as I could. Wrong solution! Yazoose Matka! Within a minute, the whole world began to spin. I was looking at two barns. I lay down in the pasture grass, looked up, and saw three bright yellow suns. My stomach felt like somebody was churning butter in there. I had to get rid of the Plow Boy. I rose to my hands and knees and not only did I get rid of the Plow Boy, I got an up close and personal look at everything I'd had for breakfast and, as they say, much, much more! I lay back down in the grass for quite a spell. Then I turned tail for home.

Throughout the coming years—even after I had become the age and size of a "grown man"—when Grampa reached for his beloved can of Plow Boy, he would sometimes give me a sideways glance. However, he never offered and I never again asked "for a little taste out of that can." Yes, Martha, that can of Plow Boy Chewing Tobacco held about as much interest for me as if it were filled with sawdust soaked in turpentine. As a matter of fact, that's a pretty fair likeness, I would say!

During the summer months, almost every day after morning chores, Grampa conducted an ongoing battle with three things.

First, after the potatoes were hilled (a hoe was used to form a small hill of ground around the potato plant), Grampa would walk through the potato patch searching for "tater bugs." The bugs were picked from the potato plants and sent to their watery grave in a half-full water pail Grampa carried about.

The underside of each potato leaf was examined, and small clusters of tater bug eggs soon joined their parents in the water pail as well. So now the bugs, which had intended to eat the leaves off the potato plants, were eaten by the chickens. When the tater bug pail was dumped near the chicken coop, Grampa looked on with a certain sense of satisfaction as the chicken flock devoured thei midsummer-day dinner.

At noon, he would go into the house to sit down with Granny at the big oak kitchen table for a hot, home-cooked dinner.

After dinner, he retired to the front porch for some much-needed rest. His idea of rest, however, involved the second of his three-pronged daily attack upon common farm pests, namely flies. Flies of any size, shape, age, or color. Face flies, deerflies, horseflies, friendly flies, and houseflies all lived in a land of great danger when they entered Grampa's domain. In particular, his front porch. Let's just say he had an extremely low tolerance for flies in general.

As a matter of fact, his name was held in the highest regard among hill folk when talk turned to the killing of flies. Word of his amazing feats of endurance, tenacity, patience, perseverance, and numbers killed had spread far and wide.

It was his weapon of choice, however, that elevated him to legendary status. Through countless hours of trial and error, untold numbers of designs, and many failures, he had finally triumphed. Grampa had perfected and created—using his native wit and intelligence, along with a deep hatred for flies—the mother of all flyswatters! It was an awesome thing.

The handle was about three feet long and crafted from quarter-inch wrought iron with a six-inch loop handle on one end for his huge, gnarly hand. The other end was heated and flattened and had some holes drilled through it. A piece of rubber truck-tire inner tube, about ten inches long and six inches wide, was punched through with many holes to reduce wind resistance. The rubber swatter was then carefully stitched onto the flat part of the iron handle using double-thickness, black, braided fishing line. It was a work of art. A diabolically created masterpiece. An efficient weapon even in the hands of a rank amateur. One could have carried the thing in bear country with a good chance of warding off the most vicious of attacks.

Just inside the front porch from the kitchen door, above the wood box, hanging from a sizeable nail was the "Brute," as Grampa's invention came to be known.

After dinner, he would take it down from its rightful place of honor. Then, as if he were stalking a white-tailed deer, he began to patrol every inch of the eighty-foot, L-shaped, screened-in porch that ran along two sides of the big square house.

Whoosh. Ka whop. The Brute had been brought to bear! It could be heard from anywhere in the farmyard as well as in any room of the house. Every fly within earshot knew there was a 99 percent chance that one of its comrades had fallen.

Grampa possessed a certain finesse, an accuracy, a delicate yet deadly touch unequaled anywhere in the hills. With a mere flick of the wrist, he would leave a dead fly lying on its back, legs sticking up, upon the porch floor. His unorthodox sidearm delivery was known to reduce a perfectly normal, healthy fly to a tiny grease spot. Grampa's most famous technique, however, was the one he called the "Bunch Swat."

This was accomplished by finding a place where two or more flies were gathered. Timing was everything. When the flies were grouped to his liking, he would slowly raise the Brute over his head, poised in midair. Poised. Waiting. Now, before an eye could blink, the Brute came flying forward and down in an overhead swing like that used to split firewood. The resulting carnage was, at times, beyond belief. To the best of my knowledge, Grampa's all-time record was a seven-fly Bunch Swat.

After an hour or so of porch patrol, every fly that was not lying belly-up on the windowsills and the porch floor or turned into a grease spot against the window screens had gone into deep hiding of a fearful nature.

This called for a change in tactics. Grampa would now lie down—always on his back—upon the tattered, old, stuffed horsehair couch next to the wood box. The Brute lay across his chest, always at the ready. Grampa's eyes were closed, his breathing slow and measured, and now and then a snore would escape his half-open mouth. In all outward appearances, one would think he was fast asleep.

He was, however, a master of deception. Perhaps this was just another ploy to entice some poor, battle-fatigued fly to emerge from its hiding place. One thing is certain. During the next hour, the Brute would not lie in complete silence.

After his "rest" period, Grampa would sweep the windowsills and the porch floor. The resulting heap of fly cadavers resting in the dustpan could, at times, stagger even the most vivid imagination. Grampa would nod in silent approval as he dumped them into the slop pail.

Then it was out to the tool shop, where he gathered up his razor-sharp, long-handled hoe and his trusty weed sprayer to continue his battle with the third common farm pest: It was time to go after the "tissles." Everything from Canada thistles to bull thistles—indeed, any plant that resembled a thistle met the same end. It was chopped off a little above ground level. The stump, including any leaves, was sprayed with weed killer—the makeup of which I do not know. I believe a single application, however, would have removed several layers of varnish from a board.

The sprayer held about three gallons of weed killer.

A small handle on top of the sprayer was used to pump air pressure into the tank. A rubber hose ran from the tank to a brass nozzle, which had a small handle. When pressed, this handle released a fine spray of weed killer onto the hoed-off stubble. Grampa carried the sprayer over his shoulder on a canvas strap.

In one respect, "goin' after the tissles" was easier than dispatching tater bugs or walloping flies with the Brute, for the simple reason that the aforementioned were mobile. The thistles were rooted in one place. However, they were spread over twenty-eight acres of land.

The cow pasture was of top concern. Thistles posed a problem with the growing of grass and the grazing of cattle.

Day after day, week after week, as the late-afternoon summer sun beat down upon him, Grampa walked the cow pasture. Up the hill behind the barn, down past the hayshed meadow, over along the crick, on and on he went. Looking.

Always looking for that one miserable thistle, which if missed could grow a seed head and spread its evil children to the four winds.

Then it was time for supper and, afterward, his cow-milking chores. In late evening, we would gather on the porch. Granny in her rocking chair squeaked a steady rhythm, while Grampa and I sat on the porch couch. The tinkle of the cowbell drifted from the hayshed meadow. Crickets felt the pulse of a hot summer's night. A whippoorwill told of the darkness soon to come.

Granny's summer days were also spent doing a host of chores. She was always the first one up in the morning. A kerosene-soaked corncob, along with dry kindling, was used to start a fire in the kitchen range. The big old cookstove was about six feet long and three feet wide. On one end was the firebox. Next were four removable lids: round iron discs, each with a slot for a one-fits-all handle. Then a flat grill and, finally, a water reserve tank—or, in today's lingo, a water heater. There were two warming ovens above the main stove and a baking oven below. The kitchen range was used every day of the year.

In the summer, Granny kept the windows closed and the shades down. A row of trees grew along the west side of the house. Their shade was the only form of "air conditioning" the old folks ever knew.

After Granny had cooked and served breakfast, she took water from the cookstove tank to wash dishes.

Chicken feeding was next. "Here, chick, chick, chicky," she'd call and the free-ranging chickens would gather 'round her as she cast handfuls of cracked corn and oats on the ground.

There was always firewood to bring to the house from the woodshed. Dinner and supper to cook. Clothes to wash by hand. The house to clean. Flower beds to tend. Clothes to be patched and darned and mended. Bolts of cloth to be made into new clothes on her treadle sewing machine. Garden produce to pick and put up in quart- and pint-sized glass jars, which were cooked a dozen or more at a time in a copper wash boiler. This was called canning, although it had absolutely nothing to do with "cans" as we know them today.

At times, when Grampa complained how hard he worked, Granny would bring him up short by reciting an old hill country saying: A man works from sun to sun, but a woman's work is never done!

In mid- to late August, it was time to take to the woods again. Berry picking time. The blackberry patches held great bounty for us. Walking sticks were taken up and shoulder bags hoisted. Karo syrup pails of the one-gallon kind hung from leather belts around our waists.

Grampa fired up the old Chevy and bounced and coughed and smoked his way along the field road, always uphill toward the woods. He was, however, riding alone.

Granny and I trudged behind him on foot. She said, "It's safer for us to walk, on account of if we rode along, we might take Grampa's attention off his drivin'."

Finally, Gramps brought the old metal monster to a skidding, belching stop just inside the woods. We each took our empty syrup pails, shoulder bags, and walking sticks from the car and headed uphill into the blackberry patch.

The berry patch was a tangled maze of prickly, twisted canes. The berries were juicy and plump, the size of the end of a grown man's thumb. At first, more berries went into our mouths than into the pails on our belts. When my one-gallon syrup pail was full, I'd fight my way out of the patch and dump it into the big pail. When the big pail was full, it was carried to the car.

I was often warned to look, listen, and tap the ground ahead with my walking stick in the berry patch. Two things were a danger to berry pickers: rattlesnakes and ground-nesting bees, otherwise known as yellow jackets. Both would usually warn you if they knew you were coming. The snakes would rattle, and the bees would buzz and rise up from the ground. This allowed you to backtrack and go to a different berry patch.

By late afternoon, we headed back down to the farmyard to wash the berries. I once asked Granny how it was that she could go through a berry patch wearing her long dress and come out with fewer cuts and scratches than Grampa or I did.

"'Cause of the difference between men and women," she said. "A woman knows enough to ease herself through between the canes and reach gently for the berries, to have a little patience. A man rams into that berry patch. He's got canes and stalks wrapped around him, and he grabs onto them berries like they're gonna run away on him. Reminds me of a bull got turned loose in a small chicken coop. Awful sight, it is."

Granny made jelly and jam out of most of the berries. Grampa took the rest for wine makin' in big crock jugs. When the wine was done "workin'," Grampa poured it into wooden keg barrels down in the cellar.

When Jack Frost began to form his etchings upon the morning grasses, the squirrels and chipmunks started to practice their layaway plan for winter. We followed suit. Hickory nuts picked from the forest floor by the bushel basketful were stored in the attic. These were saved for the long nights of winter, when we cracked the nuts with a small hammer and used a nut pick to free the meat from the shells.

Picking wild apples was generally the last autumn gathering job.

Winter brought much darkness to the big, square farmhouse. Grampa and Granny had never hooked up to the electric lines that ran through the valley. From the center of the kitchen ceiling hung a single, bare light bulb of low wattage, powered by a home light plant. This was a small gasoline engine, which charged several large batteries in the basement. Therefore, the "electric system" was used very little. Kerosene lamps were still in full use.

When the white winds of winter howled out their woes, we gathered in the kitchen to crack nuts, pop corn in an old fire-blackened shaker pan, and share a bottle of soda pop or a glass of Grampa's homemade wine.

My brother, Gerry, and I sat quietly and listened while our parents and the old folks told and retold stories of years ago.

It was, however, Granny who held center stage when it came to storytelling. She sat by the kitchen table. A gray thatch of hair hung low on her forehead. Lantern shadows crossed her weathered face, and her dark eyes flashed and sparkled as she told of her early childhood.

Her family's Indian friends paddled canoes from the Mississippi up the Buffalo River and always stopped by to trade beautiful beadwork and handmade baskets for farm goods.

Granny told of how thieves had come to steal a pig in the middle of a rainy, windy night so the horses couldn't be heard. In the morning, wagon-wheel tracks were visible and a pig was missing.

Once, her father had been sick for several days. All home remedies had failed. That night, the family helped him get astride a horse and he rode sixteen miles to the nearest doctor, where, as Granny liked to say, "That sawbones cut him open for appendix trouble." Her pa had to stay there for two weeks till he could ride the horse home.

Granny often recounted how much she liked going to school. And how she had to quit after the third grade "on account of workin' on the farm." She would tell us, "Your Grampa was lucky. He got to go through the eighth grade."

Both Grampa and Granny spoke English with a thick accent. "Low Dutch," a German/Swiss language, was what they spoke most of the time. It would naturally follow that they could twist and contort normal words in such a fashion as to send any respectable English teacher over the edge in short order.

One of Grampa's favorites was "squeen" for window screen: "I mashed that old fly plumb up against the squeen." "Tissle" meant thistle: "I went after the tissles all afternoon." "Shimney" stood for chimney: "Got to clean out the shimney."

Granny had her favorites, too. "Wissit" passed for visit: "We went there on a wissit." She said "callander" for calendar: "Never go fishin' without lookin' at the callander to see if it's a fish day. When the dark fish form is there they'll bite."

Her most famous word twist was "Kegapee" instead of Kewpee. On the rare occasions when Grampa and Granny went to Winona, Minnesota, they would usually stop at a little family restaurant called the Kewpee to splurge on an eat-out meal. More than one person's eyebrows twitched and their mouths fell agape when Granny asked them if they ever ate at the Kegapee.

The years slipped away all too quickly, and Grampa and Granny began, ever so slowly, to slip away with them.

However, Grampa and Granny never abandoned their hill country lifestyle. They used the kitchen range for cooking, got their water from the hand pump, and still went outside to use the two-holer outhouse. Neither of them ever needed a pair of full-time eyeglasses; their reading glasses came from the dime store.

Grampa passed away peacefully in his own bed in the big, old, square farmhouse at the age of eighty-eight.

For a while after Grampa was gone, Granny was forced to use a metal walker because of her bum leg. Even this did not remove the twinkle from her eyes, nor did it dampen her sharp wit.

She often remarked, "That old walker is a right handy fishin' tool. I can lean on it, hang a can of worms from it, and lay my big cane pole across it. Never have to stoop over at all."

Granny spent a year and a half short of a century upon this Earth.

These days, I sometimes go to the little hill country farm where I was born. My nephew, Tim, and his wife, Jo, live there now. I walk to the edge of the hill where the barn once stood, close my eyes, and I'm once again knee-high to a grasshopper.

I shuffle through the dusty cow yard in summertime to follow a cow path down the hill among scattered burr oaks to a lush pasture of long ago. Here I follow the clear, happy waters of Yeager Valley Crick, hoping to see a fish dart to the safety of an undercut bank. Grasshoppers leap in terror at my approach, while leopard frogs do high dives from bank to crick.

I find those old familiar stepping stones across the crick and take that final jump to the opposite bank. Then I crawl under a barbed-wire fence into Grampa and Granny's meadow pasture to walk a cow trail up to their little barn.

I open a rough board gate and go up the garden path to open the creaky front-porch door.

"Hey, Boobily." Grampa swings his stiff, arthritic legs to the floor from the tattered porch couch and pats a seat by his side. "Sit down by your old Grampa for a spell."

His gnarled, twisted hands grip the Brute flyswatter. "They're thick as hair on a dog today," he says. He points the swatter at a smattering of dead flies lying on the porch floor.

We talk of the weather, crops, cows, and fishing.

He says it's gonna rain 'cause his bones hurt him and how he's going after the tissles this afternoon.

I get up and go past the wood box into the kitchen.

Granny is tending to her cooking and baking by the kitchen range. I run to her and bury my head in her apron, and she puts her arms around me. The wonderful odor of wood smoke, a hint of sweat, and fresh-baked bread finds my nose. We talk of the garden, flowers, fishing, and whether I'll like school in the fall.

Grampa comes in, and the three of us lunch a little on home-smoked summer sausage, bread, and Granny's saucer-sized sugar cookies.

We say our goodbyes, and I close the front porch door behind me to retrace my steps toward home.

I often wish I could return to those long-ago days.

I guess I have in a way, haven't I?

ABOUT THE AUTHOR

Kenny Salwey is a woodsman who has spent his life in the backwaters of the Mississippi River. He is the author of *The Last River Rat* and *Kenny Salwey's Tales of a River Rat* and the narrator of the award-winning wildlife documentary *Mississippi: Tales of the Last River Rat*. A popular nature speaker since 1988, Kenny  travels the upper Midwest talking to groups about his life in the river bottoms and about the cycles of nature.

Kenny and his wife, Mary Kay, live outside Alma, Wisconsin. He also maintains two remote shacks in the Whitman Swamp.

Photograph courtesy of Sandra Lines